YORK NOTES

The Prologue to The Canterbury Tales

Geoffrey Chaucer

Notes by Michael and Mary Alexander

Longman

York Press

YORK PRESS
322 Old Brompton Road, London SW5 9JH

PEARSON EDUCATION LIMITED
Edinburgh Gate, Harlow,
Essex CM20 2JE, United Kingdom
Associated companies, branches and representatives throughout the world

First published 1999
Third impression 2002

ISBN 0-582-41458-X

The portrait of Chaucer on p. 93 is from The Ellesmere Manuscript Facsimile
Edition 1911 (Private Collection) and is published by permission of The
Bridgeman Art Library, London/New York

Designed by Vicki Pacey, Trojan Horse, London
Phototypeset by Gem Graphics, Trenance, Mawgan Porth, Cornwall
Colour reproduction and film output by Spectrum Colour
Produced by Pearson Education North Asia Limited, Hong Kong

C ONTENTS

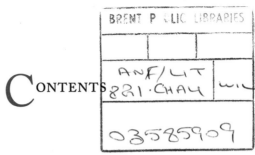

PART ONE

INTRODUCTION

HOW TO STUDY A NARRATIVE IN VERSE

Studying a verse narrative in medieval English on your own requires self-discipline and a carefully thought-out plan of work.

- You will need to read this short work more than once. Read it through first for pleasure, and then read it more slowly and thoroughly.
- Read the poem aloud in an imitation (however bad) of the historically appropriate pronunciation. (If possible, try to listen to a recording.) By practising thus, and sounding the final -*e* when the **metre** suggests it, metre and rhythm can be found (see Textual Analysis). This helps with understanding the meaning and the tone of what is said.
- Look up the meanings of all the words you do not know. Some words which survive into modern English have changed their senses. Some may use more than one meaning. Some require notes to explain them.
- On a second or a third more careful reading, make detailed notes on the characters, and on subjects which recur in the narrative. Further readings will help you memorise details and will develop new thoughts.
- In the early stages of studying a text of this kind, it is better to read part or whole of the poem aloud than to read critics. First try to make parts of the poem familiar to your eye, ear and memory. Then you are in a position to discuss the text with others or to read criticism critically.
- Divide the narrative into its principal parts and see whether the narrator plays the same role in each of these parts.
- Is the narrator's point of view one which we are supposed to accept at all times?
- Do some ideas and values come up again and again? If so, do these need to be explained by reference to historical beliefs or different social and cultural situations?
- In exams or essays, support your argument with brief quotations or details of the text. Try to find your own quotations: it makes the essay so much more interesting for the examiner!
- Always express your own ideas in your own words.

This York Note offers an introduction to the text and cannot substitute for close reading and a critical study of secondary sources.

The Prologue, also known as the General Prologue, forms the introduction to *The Canterbury Tales*, which has become the most popular work of the most popular English writer of the Middle Ages, Geoffrey Chaucer. In it Chaucer tells us how one April he was staying a night at the Tabard Inn in Southwark, meaning to begin his pilgrimage to Canterbury next morning, when a company of pilgrims came in, and he joined them. He then describes each of the pilgrims in turn, in a set of portraits which remains the most famous extended piece of character-drawing in English. It is done in an entertaining and informal way. The pilgrims all agree to a proposal by the Innkeeper that they should take part in a game: each is to tell a tale on their ride towards the shrine of St Thomas of Canterbury. This general introduction to *The Tales* as a whole makes sense on its own. In only 858 lines, the Prologue offers a brilliantly coloured, animated and detailed picture of English social life in action.

Geoffrey Chaucer, who died in 1400, is the first famous English poet. There had been English poems for 700 years before him, the Old English eighth-century epic poem *Beowulf* for example. But Chaucer is the only medieval English poet known to most later poets. He perfected a new kind of verse in English, the five-beat, ten-syllable line used by Shakespeare – and Milton, Pope, Wordsworth, Tennyson, Eliot and Heaney – and still in use. He is also the only English poet to have been read continuously since the Middle Ages, surprising and delighting new readers in each generation.

S<small>OCIAL HISTORY</small>

Some lasting impressions of the Middle Ages come from the General Prologue – pilgrims on horseback, the *parfit gentil* Knight, the hunting Monk, the lady Prioress, the thin Clerk of Oxford, the Pardoner selling his fake relics, the Wife of Bath looking for her sixth husband, the Miller looking for a fight, the ideal Parson, the good Ploughman. The pilgrimage begins in a tavern in Southwark, and is to end in Canterbury Cathedral. Pubs and churches are institutions which England inherits from the Middle Ages. The company of pilgrims is linked by good fellowship and the excitement of a spring outing. The pilgrimage to the shrine of St Thomas à Becket at Canterbury was the most popular in

England. The pilgrims go to seek the holy martyr who has helped them when they have been sick, but many of them are also on holiday. The Prologue is a comprehensive picture and full of life. It is the first page in English social history, rich in detail and colour. As the seventeenth-century poet John Dryden said of Chaucer's men and women: 'Here is God's plenty! We have our forefathers and great-grand-dames all before us, as they were in Chaucer's days.'

The liveliness of the Prologue owes much to Chaucer's eye for personal detail, his sense of humour and his style. It was a good idea to give a miscellany of stories the form of a story-telling competition, and a better one to make the tellers a group of pilgrims riding along a road. It was a stroke of genius to have twenty-nine pilgrims be so kind as to include him, their creator, in their company. At the Tabard he speaks to each of them and becomes one of their company. By speaking to him, they speak to us.

The General Prologue is a lovely text, fresh and unacademic. But it is also packed with social detail which needs some study if it is to be fully appreciated. And Chaucer's English, though it is largely intelligible, also needs a little study to bring out its meaning, implication and flavour. This is a short but richly rewarding text.

PART TWO

COMMENTARIES

NOTE ON THE TEXT

The text of the General Prologue is found in all complete manuscripts of *The Canterbury Tales*. There are more than eighty manuscripts of the *Tales*, the text of which breaks up into ten Fragments. The major manuscripts begin with the Prologue, part of the *First Fragment*. No manuscript seems to date from Chaucer's lifetime, but two manuscripts with a full run of tales, known as the Ellesmere Manuscript and the Hengwrt Manuscript, are dated within ten years of Chaucer's death in 1400. These are regarded as close to Chaucer's texts and are the basis of modern editions, though editors also take readings from later fifteenth-century manuscripts. Medieval texts differ from manuscript to manuscript. The Ellesmere is handsomely illustrated with miniature portraits of the pilgrims and of Chaucer (reproduced in *The Canterbury Tales: Illustrated Prologue*, ed. Michael Alexander, Scala Books, 1996). *The Canterbury Tales* were first printed by William Caxton in 1477, and have been reprinted in every century since then.

There is currently no single edition of the Prologue on its own. The edition used as a basis for the present book is *The Canterbury Tales: the First Fragment*, edited by Michael Alexander, Penguin, 1996. This has the text of the General Prologue in a helpful format with, on facing pages, a very full glossary. Besides the General Prologue, it contains the other parts of the First Fragment of Chaucer's *Tales*: the Knight's Tale, the Miller's Tale, the Reeve's Tale, and their Prologues, a total of 4420 lines in all. It also has an introduction, and full notes.

The standard single-volume edition of Chaucer's complete works is *The Riverside Chaucer,* third edition, edited by Larry D. Benson, Oxford University Press, Oxford, 1988. The text is in double columns, with glosses at the foot of the page and an excellent full glossary at the back. It has good introductions and very full and scholarly notes. A handy edition of *The Canterbury Tales* is edited by A.C. Cawley, Dent, London, 1958, revised Malcolm Andrew, 1996, with marginal glosses but with few of the notes which are especially useful for the General Prologue. There are many editions of *The Canterbury Tales*, complete and selected, and of individual tales and groups of tales.

Many students use translations. But translations tend to substitute for the original, and it is dangerous to rely on them in preparing for examinations. Good examination answers quote the original text, and the translation will often give the wrong sense. Translations of verse into verse inevitably misrepresent the sense as well as the music of their originals. This is particularly the case when translating from an earlier stage to a later stage of the same language, as the translator cannot avoid using modern English words descending from the words in the original, though the modern word will often have changed sense (see the discussion of the portrait of the Prioress – Textual Analysis, Text 2). Chaucer is full of nuances and little jokes which are also lost in translation. Finally, a translation is not necessary, for Chaucer's English in the General Prologue, a short text, is not difficult and can be enjoyed after very little study by any speaker of English – or of French, German, Flemish, Dutch or other European languages. The authors of this note advise students to avoid translations of the Prologue.

Suggestions for further reading are found in Part Six.

SYNOPSIS

The Prologue has three parts: a short introduction, the series of portraits of the pilgrims, and their consent to the Host's proposal of a tale-telling game.

Chaucer tells how, at the Tabard Inn in Southwark on the night before his pilgrimage to the shrine of Thomas à Becket in Canterbury, he fell in with a company of twenty-nine pilgrims. These he describes in some detail, in the famous series of portraits. He follows the conventional division of medieval society into 'estates' and introduces them in the usual order: the military estate, the clerical estate, and the estate of the workers (Latin *pugnatores, oratores, laboratores*: fighters, prayers and workers). This last estate has the most pilgrims, introduced roughly in order of social precedence. Chaucer ends with a group of rogues, mentioning himself last.

At the suggestion of the Host of the Tabard, they agree to tell two tales on the way to Canterbury and two on the way back to London; the best tale is to earn its teller a free supper at the Tabard on their return. The pilgrims accept the Host as judge of the tale-telling game. When they set out next morning, the pilgrims draw lots to decide who shall tell the first tale, and the Knight wins. The Prologue ends with the Knight about to start his tale.

A brief account of the rest of the *First Fragment* and a briefer sketch of the rest of the *Tales* may be of use. The Knight's noble tale of Palamon and Arcite is admired, particularly by the nobler pilgrims, and the Host invites the Monk, as senior churchman, to tell the next tale. However, the Miller, who is already drunk, insists instead on telling a bawdy story about the cuckolding of a carpenter. The Reeve, who is also a carpenter, angrily answers with a bawdier story about a miller. The Cook then begins on a still bawdier tale of an apprentice and a prostitute, but the *First Fragment* of the Tales ends when the Cook has scarcely begun.

This pattern of solemnity followed by comic and even ribald chaos is echoed in more than one of the remaining nine Fragments of the *Tales*, in which twenty-two more pilgrims tell their varied stories, including Chaucer himself (who tells two) and the Parson, whose tale, a long treatise on Christian penitence, ends the collection. *The Canterbury Tales* thus comes to an end before Canterbury is reached, and before the tale-telling competition has completed the first of its four stages.

The Canterbury Tales, then, is incomplete, perhaps because of the poet's death, although other works of his are unfinished. But the shape of the work is clear. As in other medieval collections of popular stories, such as the Arabian *Thousand and One Nights* or the *Decameron* by Boccaccio, an older Italian writer whom Chaucer may have met, the primary story forms a convenient framework to a miscellany of many different kinds of tales: romances, fairy stories, bawdy tales, sermons, saints' lives, beast-fables, **allegories**. However, this **frame-story**, as it is sometimes called, has a life of its own. Some of the tales are dramatic expressions of the characters of their tellers, and the events of the pilgrimage are sometimes of greater interest and significance than the tales. Human life was often thought of as a pilgrimage, an **image** which gives Chaucer's work a **symbolic** meaning of a kind very common in the Middle Ages.

The General Prologue (so called to differentiate it from prologues to individual tales) is the general narrative introduction to *The Canterbury Tales* as a whole. It sets the scene in spring, the season of pilgrimages, and introduces Chaucer as a pilgrim at the Tabard Inn. Then follows the series of portraits of individual pilgrims, from the Knight down to the Pardoner. Finally we meet the Host and hear his proposal for the tale-telling competition. The next morning the pilgrimage sets out.

Detailed commentaries

Introduction (lines 1–42)

Lines 1–18   Formal opening

In the spring, when flowers grow and birds sing, people long to go on pilgrimage, and the English particularly love to go to Canterbury, the shrine of St Thomas.

> Medieval romances often open with an evocation of spring, but Chaucer's description is scientific, astronomical and classical, and his first long sentence is elaborate and formal (see Textual Analysis, Text 1).

1 **shoures** showers
  soote sweet, gentle
2 **droghte** dryness
3 **veyne** vein, vessel of sap
  swich licour liquid such
4 **Of which vertu** that by its power
  engendred generated
  flour flower
5 **Zephirus** god of the west wind
  eek also

FORMAL OPENING (LINES 1-42) continued

6 **Inspired** breathed life into

holt wood

heeth field

7 **croppes** the growth of leaf (*not* crops of wheat or barley)

yonge young (Aries is the first sign in the solar year)

8 **Ram** the sign of Aries

half cours the second half of its course

9 **foweles** birds

10 **ye** eye

11 **So ... corages** so much does Nature prick them in their hearts

12 **longen folk to goon** people long to go

13 **palmeres** pilgrims (those going to Jerusalem wore a palm)

straunge strondes foreign shores

14 **ferne ... londes** remote shrines known in various lands

15 **shires ende** corner of (each) county

16 **wende** make their way

17 **blisful martir** blessed martyr. Thomas Becket (also Thomas à Becket and St Thomas of Canterbury) died as a witness to the Christian faith in 1170, put to death in Canterbury Cathedral by knights of Henry II of England. Becket had been Lord Chancellor, the chief officer of state, but when he became Archbishop of Canterbury, the head of the Church in England, he defended the Catholic Church against the king. Canterbury, two days' ride from London into Kent, immediately became one of the chief places of pilgrimage in Europe

seke seek

18 **holpen** helped (a saint can intercede with God for sick people who pray to him)

seeke sick (identical rhyme)

LINES 19–42   At the Tabard

Chaucer joins a company of pilgrims staying at the same inn as himself.

How does Chaucer get to know the pilgrims, and what is their reaction to him?

19 **Bifil** it happened, befell

20 **Southwerk** the parish on the south bank of the Thames opposite the City of London, to which it was linked by London Bridge

20 **Tabard** Tabard Inn, a hostelry, bearing the name of a short armorial coat

    as I lay while I was staying

22 **corage** spirit

25 **sondry** various sorts

    aventure chance

28 **wyde** spacious

29 **esed** accommodated

    atte beste in the best way

30 **shortly** in short

    to reste setting

31 **hem everichon** every one of them

32 **anon** soon

33 **made forward** (we) made agreement

    erly for to ryse to rise early

34 **ther ... devyse** in the way I shall recount to you

36 **Er that** before

37 **Me thynketh it** it seems to me

38 **condicioun** state, circumstances

40 **which** of what occupation

    degree social rank

THE PORTRAITS OF THE PILGRIMS (LINES 43–746)

LINES 43–78   The Knight

Heading the military estate is the Knight, a professional soldier, and a devout example of Christian chivalry and of the military virtues. He has fought honourably both for his earthly lord and for the Lord of all Christians, campaigning along the whole frontier between Christendom and *hethenesse*, from Southern Spain right round the whole east end of the Mediterranean and also eastward along the Baltic coast into Russia. Despite his prowess and his undefeated record, he was humble and courteous – a true, complete and noble knight (line 72). He offers thanks for his safe return from campaigning by going on pilgrimage.

The knight's virtues and his roll-call of campaigns recall the ideals of the twelfth-century Crusades: expeditions to regain the

Holy Land from the Muslims, led by knights from northwest Europe. The Knight has fought only against Muslims, heathens and schismatics, not (as his real-life contemporaries had done) against fellow Catholics in France and Spain. He is a superlative example of a type virtually extinct in Chaucer's day. That may be part of Chaucer's point. Each pilgrim is a superlative example of his type. If the Knight's achievements are checked against dates and places, they seem too good to be true. But Chaucer was drawing an ideal.

43 **worthy** of proven valour and virtue

45 **riden out** go on campaign

46 **Trouthe** integrity, fidelity to obligation

fredom noble generosity

curteisie courteous conduct

48 **therto** moreover

ferre further

49 **As wel ... hethenesse** as much in Christian as in nonChristian lands

51 **Alisaundre** Alexandria (Egypt), taken in 1365 by Christian knights under Peter of Lusignan, King of Cyprus and sixth Latin king of Jerusalem

52 **Ful ... bigonne** many a time had he taken the head of the table (the place of honour)

53 **Pruce** Prussia, seat of the Teutonic Knights

54 **Lettow** Lithuania, which followed its Prince Jagiello into the Catholic Church in 1386

reysed campaigned

Ruce Russia

55 **degree** rank

56 **Gernade** Granada, the Moorish province in southern Spain

57 **Algezir** Algeciras, taken in 1344, whereafter the Benmarin dynasty returned to their kingdom in Southern Morocco (Belmarye), where Christian knights also campaigned

58 **Lyeys** Ayas, Armenian port near Antioch, in modern Turkey

Satalye Attalia, in Armenia

59 **Whan** when (Peter of Cyprus took them in 1367 and 1361 respectively)

Grete See Mediterranean

60 **armee** military expedition

62 **oure feith** Christianity

Tramyssene Tlemçen, Western Algeria

63 **lystes** in a tournament or formal combat of champions

ay always

65 **Palatye** Balat in modern Turkey (ancient Miletus). An emir of Balat was a vassal of Peter of Cyprus

66 **Agayn** against

67 **And ... prys** and always he had an outstanding reputation

68 **worthy** brave

wys wise, discreet

69 **port** bearing

70 **vileynye** rudeness

71 **maner wight** kind of person

72 **verray** true (*not* very)

parfit complete

gentil noble

74 **His hors ... gay** his horses were good, but he was not gaily dressed himself

75 **fustian** coarse cotton cloth

gypon tunic

76 **bismotered** marked, spotted (with rust)

habergeon hauberk, coat of mail

77 **late** recently

viage campaign

LINES 79–100   The Squire

The Knight's son is an Esquire, or candidate for knighthood; an apprentice knight in the service of a senior knight. He has fought well, across the English Channel. He is a *lovyere*, full of youth, gaiety and the qualities of spring. He also has all the courtly accomplishments and treats his father with honour.

> Compare the motives, enemies, and dress of father and son. For whose sake does each perform his feats of war? (see Characterisation, on the Military).

80 **lovyere** lover

lusty zestful (*not* lustful)

80 **bacheler** probationer for the honour of knighthood (the candidate had to win his spurs by passing military and religious tests)

81 **lokkes ... presse** locks as curly as if they had been in curlers

83 **of evene lengthe** well-proportioned

84 **delyvere** agile

85 **chyvachie** cavalry expedition

86 **In ... Pycardie** in Flanders, in Artois and Picardy. These parts of modern France and Belgium across the Channel from Kent were provinces claimed by England in its Hundred Years War which had begun in 1338. Chaucer had fought in France in 1359

87 **And ... space** and conducted himself so well in such a short time

89 **Embrouded** embroidered (of his clothing)

meede meadow

91 **floytynge** playing the flute

94 **koude** knew how to

95 **endite** compose words to songs

96 **Juste** joust in a tournament

purtreye portray, draw

97 **hoote** hotly

nyghtertale night-time

98 **sleep** slept

nyghtyngale the bird of love (compare line 11)

100 **carf** carved (the meat): one of the duties of an Esquire

LINES 101–17   The Yeoman

The Knight's only follower is a yeoman, a word which in the next century came to mean a small landholder. The Knight's yeoman was obliged to follow the Knight to war. He is a forester by calling, as his *takel* shows, and had perhaps been an archer in the French wars; his six-foot longbow had a range of 265 metres. He wears a medal of St Christopher, the patron saint of foresters.

> The Yeoman is picturesque but anonymous, as are his lord and his lord's son. Are the military trio individuals or types or ideals? If ideals, ideals of what? What unites them and what divides them? (see Characterisation, on The Military).

102 **hym liste** it pleased him

103 **he** the yeoman

104 **pecok** peacock; the arrow was trimmed with peacock feathers to guide its flight

107 **His arwes ... lowe** his arrows did not fall short with sagging feathers

109 **not heed** close-cropped head

111 **bracer** archer's arm-guard

112 **bokeler** buckler, shield

114 **Harneised** ornamented

116 **bawdryk** baldric, belt

LINES 118–62   The Prioress

The Prioress, as head of a Priory of nuns, takes precedence in the clerical estate over the Monk. She is a lady as well as a nun, and models her manners on those of court. To keep little dogs was forbidden by the rules of some convents.

For a discussion of her portrait, see Textual Analysis, Text 2.

118 **Nonne** nun, a woman who takes religious vows

119 **symple and coy** shy and quiet

120 **ooth** oath

     but only

     Loy Eloi, Eligius, a founder of convents; also patron saint of goldsmiths

121 **Eglentyne** (French) sweetbriar. A name from romances

122 **service dyvyne** divine worship (the regular church liturgy)

123 **Entuned** intoned

     semely becomingly

124 **fetisly** gracefully

125 **Stratford** *not* Stratford-upon-Avon but Stratford, Bromley by Bow, Middlesex, where there was a Benedictine convent known to Chaucer. The Prioress's French was not Parisian, though this may not be a criticism

127 **At mete** at table (*not* meat)

     with alle indeed

130 **kepe** take care

132 **In ... lest** she took a particular pleasure in courtly behaviour

134 **coppe** cup

     ferthyng spot the size of a farthing coin

136 **after ... raughte** reached for her food
137 **sikerly** certainly
greet desport fine deportment
138 **of port** in her bearing
139 **peyned hire** took pains
countrefete cheere imitate the manner
140 **estatlich** dignified
141 **to ben ... reverence** to be esteemed worthy of respect
142 **for to speken** to speak
conscience conscience; also sensibility
143 **pitous** pitying, soft-hearted
145 **bledde** was bleeding
146 **Of smale houndes** some little dogs
147 **flessh** meat
wastel-breed cake (French *gâteau*), or fine bread
148 **soore** sorely
oon one
149 **men** someone (an impersonal construction, as with 'one')
with a yerde smerte sharply with a stick
151 **wympul** wimple, a nun's prescribed neck-covering
pynched pleated
152 **tretys** well formed
153 **thereto** moreover
154 **sikerly** indeed
155 **spanne** stretch between little finger and thumb
156 **hardily** scarcely
157 **fetys** well made
was war noticed
158 **smal** slender
159 **peire of bedes** set of beads, used for saying the Rosary, a sequence of prayers to the Virgin Mary
gauded embellished (every eleventh bead is for an Our Father, and was called a *gaud*)
160 **sheene** beautiful
161 **write** engraved, cut
crowned A a capital A (for Latin *Amor*, or for Richard II's queen, Anne

162 **'Amor vincit omnia'** 'Love conquers all' (secular) or 'Love binds all'
(religious)

164 **chapeleyne** assistant (*not* chaplain)

LINES 165–207   The Monk

The senior male cleric present is a Benedictine monk, whose religious
vows were the same as those of the Nun, though he takes a more relaxed
view of them. Monks were often caricatured as too fond of hunting and
good living.

> Chaucer says (line 183) that he said that the Monk's opinion was
> good. How can we tell that it is not good? How does Chaucer
> know that the Monk liked roast swan better than other roasts?
> What impression does the Monk seek to create by his dress and
> talk? What impression does he actually make? By what means
> does Chaucer suggest the difference? (see Characterisation, on The
> Clergy).

165 **a fair for the maistrie** a surpassingly fine one
166 **outridere** rider-out, estate supervisor
venerie hunting
167 **to been ... able** worthy to have been head of an abbey
168 **deyntee** fine
170 **Gynglen** to jingle (bells on the bridle were popular, especially with
Canterbury pilgrims)
172 **Ther ... celle** where this lord [a monk was addressed as lord or *daun,* from
Latin *dominus*] was in charge of the house
173 **reule** monastic Rule. The Rule of St Benedict (or Benet) of Norcia
(480–550) was the foundation of Western monasticism. St Maurus was
Benedict's disciple
174 **somdel streit** rather strict
175 **ilke** same
leet ... pace allowed old things [such as Rules] to pass away
176 **heeld ... space** observed the freedom of modern times
177 **yaf** gave
pulled hen plucked hen (a worthless object)
178 **hunters ... men** a traditional comment on hunters in the Bible, such as Esau

179 **recchelese** careless (of his duty)

180 **waterlees** out of water. ('A monk out of his monastery is like a fish out of water.' Benedictines take a vow of 'stability' to their own monastery)

181 **cloystre** cloister, monastery

184 **What** why

wood mad

185 **poure** stare

186 **swynken** toil

187 **Austyn** St Augustine of Hippo (354–430), Doctor of the Church, who **bit** (bid, commanded) that the religious should do manual work

served served, serviced; clerics were sometimes administrators in the world

188 **Lat Austyn ... reserved!** let Austin keep his hard work to himself

189 **he** the Monk

prikasour mounted hunter who follows the hare by its paw-prints or 'pricks'

192 **lust** pleasure

cost expense

193 **seigh** saw

purfiled trimmed at the edge

194 **grys** a grey squirrel fur

195 **festne** fasten

196 **ywroght** wrought, made

curious remarkable

197 **love-knotte** device

gretter larger

198 **balled** bald

199 **as ... enoynt** as if he had been anointed (which, if he is also a priest, he would have been)

200 **poynt** physical condition

201 **stepe** prominent

heed head

202 **stemed as ... leed** gleamed like the fire under a cauldron

204 **prelaat** senior cleric

205 **forpyned** wasted by suffering

206 **roost** roast meat (monks were forbidden to eat quadrupeds)

207 **palfrey** horse

berye berry

LINES 208–69   The Friar

A Friar (Latin *frater*, French *frère* brother) though a member of a religious community is not bound to a monastic life of prayer, but preaches the gospel in the world, living off charity. Friars were accused of abusing the freedom given them as mendicants (beggars) and travellers, and were satirised for the faults exemplified in this portrait.

> This is the longest portrait. Anti-fraternal satire (i.e., against friars), mostly written by clerics, expresses disgust at the way the friars, masters of the arts of preaching, could use them for begging. But Chaucer praises his social skill and charm, his preference for eating with the rich rather than feeding the poor.

> What is the effect of phrases such as *as seyde himself* and *he dorste make avaunt*? What use does Chaucer make of anticlimax in this portrait? (see Characterisation, on The Clergy).

208 **wantowne** lively

209 **lymytour** one licensed to beg in a limited district

solempne imposing

210 **ordres foure** (i) the Franciscans or Friars Minor, founded by St Francis of Assisi in 1210, known as the Grey Friars; (ii) the Dominicans, or Order of Preachers, founded by St Dominic in 1216, known as the Black Friars, (iii) the Carmelites, or White Friars, (iv) the Austin Friars (see note on line 187)

kan knows

211 **daliaunce** flirtatious flattery

212 **maad** arranged

213 **cost** expense

214 **post** pillar, support (see Galatians 2:9, where apostles are 'pillars' of the Church). Possibly the young women had to get married because they were pregnant by this *noble post*

215 **famulier** intimate

216 **frankeleyns** franklins, householders who were often prosperous and hospitable (see lines 331–60)

over above

contree district

217 **worthy** prosperous

218 **confessioun** the Sacrament of Confession, or Penance. Since the previous century, every Christian had been required to confess his sins once a year privately to a priest. If truly contrite, the penitent is absolved of the guilt of his sins. The Friar claims to have been empowered to absolve certain sins that the *curat* (line 219), a secular priest, had to refer to his bishop for absolution

220 **licenciat** licensed to hear confessions

223 **yeve penaunce** give a penance. (A penance is a token punishment for sin awarded after confession, as a condition of absolution. Medieval penances were often physical: a pilgrimage was a common form of penance)

224 **Ther as** in cases where
wiste hoped
pitaunce charitable donation

225 **povre** poor; all four Orders were vowed to poverty

226 **yshryve** shriven, absolved of sin

227 **he** the penitent
He ... avaunt the friar dared assert

228 **He wiste** he knew
repentaunt (repentance is prerequisite to absolution)

230 **He ... smerte** he is not able to weep (the Friar suggests), although he is deeply pained. (The sincere penitent was expected to weep. The Friar accepts money instead)

231 **preyeres** prayers (imposed as a penance)

232 **moote** are permitted

233 **typet ... farsed** cape was always stuffed

234 **wyves** women

235 **murye note** merry singing voice

236 **koude** knew how to
rote stringed instrument

237 **yeddynges** ballad romances
baar ... pris took the prize outright

238 **flour-de-lys** lily

241 **hostiler** innkeeper
tappestere a female tapster, barmaid

242 **Bet** better
lazar leper (after Lazarus)
beggestere beggar-woman (the kind of person friars should help)

244 **Acorded** suited

facultee official position

246 **honest** respectable

avaunce be advantageous

247 **swich poraille** such a poor class of people

248 **riche** rich people

vitaille victuals, food

249 **over** above

ther as wherever

250 **lowely of servyse** humble in offering his services

252a **ferme** rent

graunt licence (to beg in that district)

252b **haunt** home territory

253 **sho** shoe (a worthless object)

254 **'In principio'** (Latin) 'in the beginning' (the opening words of St John's Gospel, and a favourite greeting of mendicant friars)

255 **ferthyng** farthing, the fourth part of a penny

er before

256 **His purchas ... rente** his pickings were much better than his official income

257 **And rage ... whelp** he knew how to play, just as if he were a pup

258 **love-dayes** days fixed for settling disputes out of court, often by the arbitration of the clergy, who sometimes abused their powers

259 **cloysterer** one who lives in a cloister (like a monk, as opposed to one who lives in the world)

260 **cope** a priest's vestment

scoler student (like the Clerk in line 290)

261 **maister** Master of Arts, a dignified title, like the modern Doctor of Divinity

pope the Pope, head of the Church

262 **double worstede** extra-thick woven woollen cloth

semycope a short cape

263 **rounded ... presse** curved out like a bell from the mould (in the bell foundry)

264 **lipsed** lisped

wantownesse self-indulgence

267 **aryght** truly

268 **doon** do

    sterres stars

269 **cleped** called

LINES 270–84   The Merchant

The Merchant is neither a soldier nor a cleric, and comes first in the third estate, that of the workers, many of whom have mercantile values. He may be a member of the Merchants Adventurers or the Merchants of the Staple, the merchant guilds of the City of London who ran the trade between England and the Low Countries, especially the export of English cloth – a trade with which Chaucer would have to do in his work as a customs officer. City merchants were regarded with suspicion, especially if they traded in money as well as goods.

> The substantial Merchant impresses and mystifies Chaucer with his talk of his profits, his foreign exchange dealings and the importance of protecting shipping routes. Are we to be impressed? Is it significant that Chaucer is not able to discover his name? (see Characterisation, on Professionals).

270 **forked berd** forked beard, a bourgeois style

271 **mottelee** cloth woven with a parti-coloured figured design; perhaps the livery of the guild

    hye high (in a high saddle)

272 **Flaundryssh** Flemish

    bever beaver (fur)

274 **resons** opinions

    solempnely impressively

275 **Sownynge** tending to

    encrees increase

    wynnyng profit

276 **He wolde ... any thyng** he wanted the sea to be guarded against all hazards

277 **Middelburgh** the Staple port on the island of Walcheren in the Netherlands; across the North Sea from Orwell, near Ipswich, Suffolk, where Chaucer's family came from

278 **sheeldes** *écus*, French coins with a shield on one side. The Merchant traded in currency, which the Church considered tantamount to usury
279 **bisette** employed
280 **wiste** knew
wight creature
281 **estatly** dignified
governaunce conduct
282 **chevyssaunce** borrowing money
283 **For sothe** forsooth, truly
with alle after all
284 **noot** know not

LINES 285–308 The Clerk

The Clerk is a model university student, reading for a career in the Church. He is in minor orders.

Chaucer writes approvingly of the Clerk's books and conversation, but makes a joke about the unprofitability of philosophy. Can we draw any conclusions from this? What are the points of comparison with the Merchant's portrait? (see Characterisation, on Professionals).

285 **Oxenford** Oxford, seat of a university since the twelfth century
286 **logyk** logic, the principal subject in Arts
ygo gone, applied
287 **leene** lean
288 **And he ... undertake** and the clerk himself was not very fat, I swear
289 **holwe** hollow
sobrely gravely
290 **overeste** topmost
courtepy short cape
291 **geten hym** got himself
benefice living, post as a parish priest
292 **office** secular employment (usually administrative)
293 **hym ... have** he would rather have
heed side
294 **Twenty** a large number of manuscript volumes

294 **blak or reed** calf or sheepskin

295 **Aristotle** the Greek philosopher (384–322BC) whose works, preserved and interpreted by Arabic philosophers, revolutionised Western philosophy when in the twelfth century they reached Paris from Moorish Spain

296 **or fithele, or gay sautrie** fiddles and psalteries were popular with students

297 **philosophre** (i) philosopher or natural scientist, hence (ii) alchemist, seeker after the fabulous philosopher's stone which turned base metal into gold. A play on both senses of the word

298 **cofre** chest

299 **hente** obtain. Students often had to beg for support

301 **bisily** earnestly

     gan began

302 **hem … scoleye** those who gave him the means to study

303 **cure** care

304 **o** one

     neede needful

305 **forme** due form

306 **quyk** lively, sharp

     hy sentence elevated content

307 **Sownynge in** tending to (compare line 275)

LINES 309–30   The Sergeant of the Law

Sergeants-at-Law (*servientes ad legem*) were the king's servants in legal matters, chosen from among the senior barristers. Those of them who were not judges could act as circuit judges, like Chaucer's Sergeant, but still pleaded in the courts and could grow rich on their fees. They were criticised for their purchase of lands previously given by the king for services rendered.

One of these Sergeants was Thomas Pynchbec, who in 1388 signed a warrant for the arrest of Chaucer for debt. The possible pun in line 326 has suggested him as a source of this portrait.

> Compare the learning and conversation of the Clerk with those of the Sergeant, and the uses to which they are put. Examine the implications of lines 313, 320 and 326 (see Characterisation, on Professionals).

309 **war** cautious

310 **Parvys** Paradise, a name for the covered portico of a church, especially that of St Paul's, the cathedral of the City of London, the traditional meeting-place for lawyers and their clients

311 **of** in

313 **He semed ... so wise** he seemed to be so, for his words were so wise

314 **Justice** judge

assise assize or sitting of a court, held periodically in each county before judge and jury

315 **patente** patent, an open letter from the king

pleyn commissioun commission giving full powers

316 **science** knowledge

renoun reputation

317 **robes** given by clients in addition to their fees

many oon many a one

318 **purchasour** buyer-up of land

319 **fee symple** unrestricted ownership in law

In effect in the end result

320 **infect** invalidated (he made sure that his legal entitlement to any land he purchased was proof against legal challenge)

321 **nas** was not

323 **In termes** in exact legal terms

caas cases. English common law is 'case law', based on preceding decisions in similar cases

doomes decisions

324 **William** William the Conqueror, the Norman duke who conquered England in 1066 and established the administrative and legal system

were falle had occurred

325 **endite** write

make a thyng draw up a deed

326 **pynche** pick holes in, find fault with

327 **statut** statute, Act of Parliament

koude knew

pleyn by rote completely by heart

328 **He ... hoomly** the dress in which he rode was plain

medlee of mixed weave

329 **ceint** belt

329 **barres smalle** narrow stripes

330 **telle I no lenger tale** I say no more

LINES 331–60   The Franklin

A franklin was a country gentleman, a free man who held land direct from the Crown, without a knight's obligation to military service.

For a discussion of this portrait, see Characterisation, on Professionals and Textual Analysis, Text 3, where there is also a translation. The nature of true felicity or happiness was a question of moral philosophy which interested Chaucer. The Franklin is amusingly self-indulgent, but before we condemn him we should remember that Chaucer had been a JP and an MP, that his family were vintners (line 342), and that he presents himself as large in the waist.

332 **dayesye** daisy (literally 'day's eye'), the flower Chaucer often mentions

333 **complexioun** not facial colour but temperament or combination of 'humours', which produced it. The four humours (hot, cold, moist and dry), themselves combinations of the four elements (earth, air, fire and water), produced four complexions (melancholy, choleric, phlegmatic and sanguine). In medieval medicine, blood predominated in a *sangwyn* complexion: ruddy of face, pleasure-loving, of good digestion and 'humour'

334 **by the morwe** in the morning

a sop in wyn a piece of cake dipped in wine (a common light breakfast)

335 **wone** custom

336 **Epicurus** the austere Athenian philosopher (341–270BC), who held that pleasure, or the absence of pain, was the chief good. His 'Sons', the Epicureans, were later supposed to be gourmets or epicures

337 **pleyn delit** complete pleasure

338 **verray felicitee parfit** true and perfect happiness

340 **Julian** Julian the Hospitaller, a legendary saint famed for his hospitality

contree part of the world

341 **after oon** of one standard (the best)

342 **bettre envyned** with a better cellar

343 **mete** food

344 **flessh** meat

344 **plentevous** plenteous

345 **snewed** snowed

347 **After** according to

349 **partrich** partridge

     muwe cage

350 **breem** bream

     luce pike

     stuwe fish-pond (*not* stew)

351 **Wo was** unhappy was

     but if unless

352 **Poynaunt** piquant

     geere utensils for the table

353 **table dormant** a fixed table for hospitality (most tables were trestle)

354 **al ... day** all day long

355 **At sessions ... lord and sire** he presided over the sessions of the county court (as a Justice of the Peace; see line 314)

356 **knyght of the shire** Member of Parliament for the county

357 **anlaas** dagger

     gipser purse

358 **Heeng** hung

     morne morning

359 **shirreve** sheriff, the king's steward (reeve) in a county (shire); the most important office after the Lord Lieutenant of a county

     contour auditor of county finances

360 **vavasour** large landholder (vassal's vassal)

LINES 361–78   The Five Guildsmen

A guild was originally the fraternity of a trade, but by the fourteenth century there were also religious and social guilds. As the five tradesmen each have a different craft, the guild whose livery they wear here must be religious. Guilds were the organisms of social life in medieval cities; their property was confiscated under Edward VI in the sixteenth century.

> By what means does Chaucer manage to suggest the Guildsmen's corporate estimate of themselves? (see Characterisation, on Professionals).

361 **HABERDASSHERE** retailer of small articles of dress

362 **WEBBE** weaver

DYERE dyer of cloth

TAPYCER tapestry-maker

363 **o lyveree** the same livery or uniform

364 **greet** important

365 **geere** gear

apiked picked out, trimmed

366 **chaped** mounted. (Silver mountings were permitted by law to tradesmen of property worth £500)

367 **wroght** made

368 **everydeel** in every way

369 **burgeys** burgess, established citizen

370 **yeldehalle** guildhall, seat of city government

deys dais, platform

371 **Everich** each

kan knows

372 **shaply** suited

alderman civic officer assisting the mayor

373 **catel** property

rente income

374 **assente** testify (to their wealth)

375 **elles** otherwise

to blame blameworthy

376 **ycleped** called

377 **And goon ... bifore** and go to vigils in front of everyone. On vigils, the eves of feast days, the guild would go to its chapel (compare lines 449–50)

378 **roialliche ybore** royally carried for you (by a servant)

LINES 379–87   The Cook

The Cook retained by the guildsmen for the pilgrimage as an indication of their importance is not a very good cook, to judge by his repertoire and his ulcer. (He tells a vulgar tale and falls off his horse at the end of the pilgrimage, drunk.)

Is the *mormal* of line 386 significant? (see Characterisation, on Professionals).

379 **for the nones** for the occasion

380 **marybones** marrow bones

381 **poudre-marchant** flavouring powder

tart tart, sharp-tasting

galyngale sweet cyperus root, a spice like ginger

382 **Wel ... knowe** he knew well how to assess

Londoun ale considered the best

383 **koude ... sethe** knew how to roast and boil

384 **mortreux** a stew, the elements of which were prepared in a mortar

pye pie

385 **thoughte me** seemed to me

386 **shyne** shin

mormal a dried-up ulcer

387 **For** as for

blankmanger a mousse, of minced capon boiled in milk and sugar (*not* blancmange)

with equal to

LINES 388–410   The Shipman

The Shipman is the master of his barge, the *Maudelayne*. Dartmouth, 200 miles from London on the south coast of Devon, was a big port. The Bordeaux trade was the heart of the wine trade, Chaucer's family's business. As a customs officer, he knew about shipmen, who do not appear in other works satirising social types.

To what ends does this pilgrim devote his superlative professional skill? What is the effect of placing *ydrawe* at the end of line 396? Would we answer differently if we did not know something about Chaucer's own background? (see Characterisation, on Professionals).

388 **wonynge ... weste** dwelling far to the west

389 **woot** know

390 **rouncy** a powerful horse; or, possibly, a nag

as he kouthe as he knew how (that is, poorly)

391 **faldyng** coarse woollen cloth

392 **laas** lace, cord (like the lanyard of the Royal Navy)

395 **felawe** companion

THE SHIPMAN (LINES 388-410) continued

396 **ydrawe** (i) carried as cargo, (ii) stolen secretly

397 **Fro Burdeux-ward** coming from Bordeaux (the wine port of Aquitaine, formerly an English possession)

chapman merchant

398 **nyce** delicate

keep notice (compare the Prioress, line 142)

399 **faught** fought (with pirates)

hyer hond upper hand, victory

400 **sent ... hoom** a common practice: he drowned his prisoners

401 **craft** skill (*not* ship)

402 **hym bisides** which affected him

403 **herberwe** harbour

lodemenage pilotage. (The 'lodestar' is the North Star, which 'leads' navigators)

404 **noon swich** none like him

Hulle port in the north-east of England

Cartage Cartagena, a port in western Spain

405 **Hardy** tough

wys to undertake prudent in an undertaking

408 **Gootlond** Gotland; the Baltic island with its port, Visby

Fynystere Finisterra, Spain (*not* Finisterre, Brittany)

409 **cryke** creek, harbour

Britaigne Brittany (*not* Britain)

410 **Maudelayne** a vessel of this name is recorded in Dartmouth in 1379 and in 1391, when its master was a Peter Risshenden. A **barge** was a trading vessel of between 100 and 200 tons

LINES 411–44   The Doctor of Physic

Doctors came low on the social scale. The Physician is, even more than most of the pilgrims, a master of his art. Medicine then included other sciences such as astrology which now seem unscientific to modern Western medicine. His authorities are the ancient and the Arabic doctors.

> Is there any conclusion to be drawn from the disparity between the Doctor's immense learning and the final end to which it is put? (consider lines 441–44) (see Characterisation, on Professionals).

413 **To speke of** if we consider

414 **astronomye** astrology

415 **kepte** watched

deel deal (of time)

416 **In houres** at the astronomical hours of planetary influences upon the patient

magyk natureel astrology (which dealt with the 'natural' heavenly bodies, not with spirits, as did black magic)

417 **Wel ... ascendent** he knew well how to find the Ascendent in favourable position (The Ascendent is the Zodiacal sign rising above the eastern horizon; whether or not it is 'fortunate' depends upon the conjunction of the planets, which the Doctor foresees)

418 **ymages** talismans associated with Zodiacal signs

419 **everich maladye** every illness

420 **Were it ... drye** see note to **complexioun**, line 333

422 **praktisour** practitioner

423 **The cause ... roote** once the cause was known and the source of his disease

424 **Anon ... boote** he at once gave the sick man his remedy

426 **drogges** drugs

letuaries medical syrups

427 **For ... wynne** for each of them made the other to gain

428 **newe to bigynne** newly begun

429–34 **Esculapius** legendary father of medicine, Aesculapius, a Greek god, supposed in the Middle Ages to be the author of several books. Fourteen medical authorities follow, Greek, Arab and modern. Dioscorides wrote in the first century AD, Rufus in the second, as did Galen, the great medical authority of antiquity. Hippocrates, the founder of Greek medical science, flourished in the fifth century BC. Haly may be the Persian Hali ibn el Abbas (died 994)

432 **Serapion** Arab writer of the eleventh century

Razis Rhazes (of Baghdad)

Avycen Avicenna (of Bokhara)

433 **Averrois** Averroes (of Cordoba) – all were famous Arabian philosophers of the eleventh and twelfth centuries

433 **Damascien** may refer to the writings of two authors

Constantyn monk of Carthage who brought Arabian learning to Salerno in the eleventh century

434 **Bernard, Gatesden, Gilbertyn** modern British trio: Bernard Gordon, a Scot, Professor of Medicine at Montpellier about 1300; John of Gaddesden of Merton College, Oxford, who died in 1361; Gilbertus Anglicus lived in the thirteenth century

438 **His studie ... Bible** Doctors are often charged with materialism

439 **sangwyn** red cloth

 pers a Persian blue-grey cloth

440 **taffata** taffeta

 sendal a thin silk

441 **esy of dispence** slow to spend money

442 **that** what

 pestilence plague-time. The Black Death of 1349, which killed a third of the population of England, was the worst of four major outbreaks of bubonic plague in Chaucer's day

443 **For** as

 cordial medicine for heart; gold indeed formed part of prescriptions, but the next line is another comment on the doctor's avarice

LINES 445–76   The Wife of Bath

The Wife comes from the cloth-making neighbourhood of Bath, and is, like other pilgrims, skilful in her profession. As the widow of a guildsman, she could have an independent practice. 'Wife' means 'woman', but she has married five times, and, as she says in the Prologue to her tale, she would welcome a sixth husband.

In interpreting such details as the Wife's teeth or hat and spurs, medieval physiognomy and astrology are helpful (see Characterisation' on Professionals and Good Men). But an awareness of medieval doctrines on the place of woman is not needed to guess why the wife is so keen on pilgrimages.

445 **biside** nearby. The parish of St Michael's-juxta-Bathon was a centre of cloth-making. The weaving trade made the West Country rich

446 **somdel deef** somewhat deaf – as the result of a blow on the ear from her fifth husband, as recounted in the Wife's own Prologue

 scathe a pity

447 **haunt** skill

448 **passed** surpassed

448 **Gaunt** Ghent; like Ypres, a centre of Flemish weaving. Edward III attracted many Flemish weavers to settle in England, improving the weaving of English wool

449 **In al the parisshe ... noon** not a woman in the whole parish

450 **offrynge** Offertory, the part of the Mass when the people offer gifts. Today money is collected, but medieval people went up to the altar in order of social precedence (see line 377) with gifts of their own manufacture
bifore in front of

451 **ther dide** any woman were to do so
wrooth angry

452 **out of alle charitee** beyond thought of being charitable; angry

453 **coverchiefs** head-coverings
fyne ... of ground finely woven

454 **weyeden ten pound** weighed ten pounds (nearly 5 kilos)

456 **hosen** stockings (The Wife uses the offering as a shop window for her wares, and for herself)

457 **streite** tightly
moyste soft

458 **fair** pleasing
hewe hue

459 **lyve** life

460 **at chirche dore** in front of the church door (where all marriages took place)
fyve the number of husbands of the Samaritan woman in the Gospel

461 **Withouten** not counting
oother compaignye a hint at promiscuity

462 **nedeth nat** it is not necessary
as nowthe for the present, just now

463 **Jerusalem** (pronounced 'Jersalem'). Pilgrimages to the Holy Land were not uncommon, although in going thrice (**thries**) the Wife is excessive

464 **straunge strem** foreign river

465 **Rome** where Saints Peter and Paul were martyred
Boloigne Boulogne-sur-Mer boasted a miraculous image of the Virgin Mary

466 **Galice at Seint-Jame** the very popular shrine of St James the Greater, at Compostella, Galicia, northwest Spain
Coloigne Cologne in Germany housed the shrine of the Three Kings and of St Ursula

467 **She koude ... weye** she knew a lot about wandering along the road. (Compare the 'straight and narrow way' of Matthew 7:14)

468 **Gat-tothed** gate-toothed, with teeth widely spaced. The Wife in her Prologue associates this with Venus

469 **amblere** an ambling horse

esily in a relaxed way

sat she rides astride in the Ellesmere MS illustration. (Riding side-saddle was introduced into England by Anne of Bohemia, Richard II's first wife)

470 **Ywympled we** with a large wimple

471 **bokeler or a targe** buckler or a shield

472 **foot-mantel** a riding-skirt, or outer skirt

large ample (the skirt, not the hips)

473 **spores** spurs

474 **felaweshipe** company

carpe talk

476 **the olde daunce** (proverbial phrase) like 'all the ins and outs'

Lines 477–528   The Parson

The Parson is the ideal parish priest, free from the faults both of the regular clergy already described and of some parish priests. He cares for his flock rather than himself, and is free from the hypocrisy and greed of some of the pilgrims.

> Why is he described in terms of his virtues rather than his tastes, physique or dress? Which details of his portrait back up the claim made in its last line? (see Characterisation, on Good Men).

478 **TOUN** village

482 **parisshens** parishioners, inhabitants of his parish

483 **Benygne** gracious

485 **ypreved ... sithes** often proven

486 **Ful looth ... tithes** he was very reluctant to excommunicate for his tithes. (Laymen were obliged to give one-tenth of their income or produce to support their priest. Non-payment could mean exclusion from the sacrament of communion)

487 **But ... out of doute** but, beyond doubt, he would rather give

488 **aboute** in the parish

489 **offryng** money given at the Offertory (see line 450) at Easter supports the priest

substaunce property

490 **koude** knew how to (see Christian Comedy – Truth)

491 **fer asonder** far apart

493 **meschief** misfortune

494 **muche and lite** great and small

495 **Upon ... a staf** according to the example of early Christian pastors

498 **gospel** Matthew 5:19

499 **figure** analogy

500 **That ... do** traditional image

502 **lewed** unlearned

ruste rust, tarnish

503 **keep** notice

504 **shiten** covered in excrement

505 **Wel ... yive** it well becomes a priest to set an example

507 **sette ... hire** did not rent out his living. Absentee parsons appointed vicars and curates

508 **And leet ... myre** nor left his sheep (people) stuck in the bog (of sin)

510 **To seken ... soules** to get himself a chantry for souls. A chantry was a provision for a priest to say (or chant) a daily mass for the repose of the soul of a deceased person – an easier life than that of a country parish

511 **Or ... withholde** or to be retained by a guild (as chaplain)

512 **kepte ... folde** kept watch over his sheepfold

513 **myscarie** come to destruction

514 **mercenarie** hireling. From the parable in John's Gospel 10:12. The wolf represents the Devil

516 **despitous** contemptuous

517 **daungerous ne digne** arrogant nor haughty

518 **discreet** courteous

519 **fairnesse** attraction

520 **his bisynesse** what he worked for

521 **But** unless

522 **What so** whatever

lough estat low position

523 **snybben** rebuke

for the nonys for that reason

T<small>HE PARSON (LINES 477-528)</small> continued

524 **trowe** believe

nowher noon ys is none anywhere

525 **He ... reverence** he expected no reverence

526 **spiced** over-scrupulous

527 **loore** teaching

apostles twelve i.e., their example

528 **He taughte ... hymselve** the parson practised what he preached

L<small>INES</small> 529–41   The Ploughman

The Ploughman is as virtuous as his brother the Parson. He is a hard worker who loves God and his neighbour, serves others and pays his tithes. Although a peasant, the Ploughman is a small tenant farmer and a free man; not a serf bonded to stay on his manor.

Why are Parson and Ploughman brothers? What are the points of contrast between them and the pilgrims who precede them? (see Characterisation, on Good Men).

529 **was** 'he' is understood

530 **ylad ... fother** pulled many a cart-load of dung

531 **A trewe ... was he** he was a good hard worker. (Compare the modern English 'a good man and true')

532 **charitee** the supreme theological virtue, defined in the next lines in the words of Christ's supreme commandment

533 **hoole** whole

534 **thogh ... smerte** whether it was pleasant or painful to him

536 **and ... delve** and also dig ditches and make hedges

537 **povre wight** poor creature

538 **hire** payment

myght power

539 **tithes** tenth part of a man's produce, due to the Church

540 **propre swynk** own labour (that is, the corn from the fields he ploughed)

catel property, possessions (*not* cows)

541 **mere** mare (regarded as an inferior mount)

542 <small>REVE</small> Reeve, estate-manager

544 <small>SOMNOUR</small> Summoner (to the church court)

<small>PARDONER</small> supplier of Pardons or Indulgences

544 **MAUNCIPLE** Manciple, college servant

namo no more

LINES 545–66   The Miller

The Miller leads the rascally final group of pilgrims. A mill had the monopoly of grinding all the corn on a manor, and could charge a high price. This miller was strong and quarrelsome, which made it easier for him to abuse his monopoly.

The vices of the previous pilgrims were not obvious, nor were they criticised openly. Does the method of presentation begin to change now? What are the common elements in the similes in this portrait? (see Characterisation, on Stewards).

545 **stout** sturdy

carl churl, fellow

for the nones indeed

547 **proved** was shown

over al everywhere

ther he cam where he went

548 **ram** the prize in a wrestling match

549 **short-sholdred** broad-shouldered

knarre knot

550 **Ther ... harre** there was no door that he could not heave off its hinge

551 **at a rennyng** with a single charge

552 **berd** beard

reed red

554 **Upon ... right** right on the top of

555 **werte** wart

toft of herys tuft of hairs

556 **brustles** bristles

erys ears

557 **nosethirles** nostrils

558 **bar** carried

559 **forneys** furnace

560 **janglere ... goliardeys** gossip and a ribald talker

561 **that** his talk

561 **harlotries** dirty jokes

562 **Wel koude ... thries** he knew well how to steal corn and charge three times over

563 **thombe of golde** the proverb 'Every honest miller has a thumb of gold' means that there are no honest millers and few poor ones. The miller's thumb tested the corn and weighed out the flour

pardee by God

565 **sowne** sound

566 **therwithal he broughte** with it he accompanied

LINES 567–86   The Manciple

A manciple was a servant of a college or Inn of Court, who purchased the provisions under the direction of the cook and the steward. He is not a figure found in Estates satire.

What is the attitude to the Manciple's cheating?

567 **gentil** pleasant

temple the Middle and the Inner Temple are two of the lawyers' Inns of Court in London

568 **Of which achatours** from whom purchasers (caterers)

569 **vitaille** victuals

570 **taille** tally (notched on a tally-stick), credit

571 **algate** always

wayted paid attention

achaat buying

572 **ay biforn** always ahead

staat state, condition

573 **grace** grace, favour

574 **lewed** uneducated (*not* lewd)

wit intelligence

pace surpass

575 **heep** heap

576 **maistres** masters, lawyers who have qualified by being called to the bar

576 **mo than thries** more than thrice

577 **of** in

curious intimately interested

578 **duszeyne** dozen

579 **stywardes** stewards

581 **hym** the lord

lyve by sustain himself upon

propre good own property

582 **dettelees** without indebtedness

but ... wood unless he were mad

583 **scarsly** economically

hym list desire it might please him to desire

584 **al a shire** a whole county

585 **caas** situation

falle come about

586 **sette ... cappe** set the caps of them all (made them look silly)

LINES 587–622 The Reeve

A reeve was the bailiff or factor for an estate: an estate-manager. Like the
Manciple, he makes dishonest profits. A trained carpenter, he is later
angered by the Miller's tale against a carpenter. The Miller rides first, the
Reeve last.

> The Miller, the Manciple and the Reeve form a trio of dishonest
> stewards. Compare them as frauds and as personalities (see
> Characterisation, on Stewards).

587 **sclendre colerik** thin, angry (see note on line 333)

588 **ny** nigh, near, close

589 **His heer ... yshorn** his hair was cut round his head at the height of his ears

590 **top was dokked** top was cut short. Priests wore a tonsure, but also kept
their hair short

biforn in front

591 **lene** lean

592 **Ylyk** like

staf staff, stick

ysene to be seen

593 **Wel ... bynne** he know how to take care of a granary and a corn-bin

594 **auditour** auditor, accountant

on him wynne get the better of him

THE REEVE (LINES 587-622) continued

595 **wiste** knew

droghte ... reyn drought and rain

596 **yeldynge** yield

597 **neet** cattle

598 **swyn, his hors** swine (plural) and horses

stoor livestock

pultrye poultry

599 **governynge** control

600 **by his covenant** according to his agreement (legal deed of service)

yaf the rekenynge gave the reckoning

601 **Syn that** since

602 **brynge ... arrerage** cause him to be behind (in collecting money due to him)

603 **baillif** bailiff, steward

hierde shepherd

hyne hind, servant

604 **That ... covyne** whose trickery and treachery he [the Reeve] did not know

605 **adrad** in dread, terrified

606 **wonyng** dwelling

608 **purchace** buy (land) (see notes on lines 320 and 575)

609 **astored pryvely** provisioned secretly

611 **To yeve ... good** to give and lend him from out of [the lord's] own goods

612 **cote and hood** the coat and hood were a servant's perquisite. Thanks are due to an equal or superior

613 **myster** trade, occupation (French *métier*). The Reeve is made a carpenter in order to lend point to the Miller's tale against a carpenter

615 **stot** horse, cob

616 **pomely** dapple

highte was called

617 **surcote of pers** blue overcoat

619 **Northfolk** Norfolk, a county in East Anglia

620 **toun** village

clepen Baldeswelle call Bawdswell

621 **Tukked** tucked. His robe was hitched up round him into his girdle, as a friar's is

622 **hyndreste of oure route** hindmost of our crowd

LINES 623–68   The Summoner

A summoner summonsed accused persons to the Bishop's Court. Ecclesiastical law operated alongside civil law, and until the nineteenth century Church courts had jurisdiction over laity as well as clergy. Offences dealt with by these courts included sexual immorality, witchcraft and withholding of tithes. The Bishop's Court was presided over by an Archdeacon, who could impose fines backed by the threat of excommunication, which could lead to imprisonment by the civil authorities. So a summoner could easily extort money from the weak.

> The Summoner is personally vicious, and also corrupt in the conduct of his office; the latter is regarded with more disfavour. How should we read lines 655–662? (see Characterisation, on Ecclesiastical Villains).

624 **fyr-reed ... face** the face of a cherub, as red as fire. Although the faces of cherubs are traditionally red, the Summoner is not an angelic messenger

625 **saucefleem** pimpled (from 'salt phlegm')

    eyen narwe narrow eyes

626 **sparwe** sparrow; traditionally a lecher

627 **scalled** scaly, scabby

    piled scanty

629 **lytarge** white lead

630 **Boras** borax

    ceruce white lead

    tartre tartar

    noon not any kind

631 **byte** bite, scour

632 **whelkes** pimples

633 **knobbes** lumps

636 **crie** shout

    wood mad

640 **decree** decree (of canon law)

643 **Watte** Wat (short for 'Walter')

644 **grope** examine minutely, probe

646 **Ay ... crie** he would always call out: 'Questio quid juris'. (Latin) 'I ask which law applies to this case'

647 **gentil harlot** easy-going rascal. ('Harlot' was applied exclusively to women only in the next century)

649 **suffer** allow

for in return for

650 **have** keep, enjoy

his the fellow's (not the Summoner's)

651 **atte fulle** at the end (of the year)

652 **a fynch ... pulle** pluck the feathers of a finch (seduce a girl)

653 **owher** anywhere

a good felawe a good companion

655 **ercedekenes curs** archdeacon's curse, excommunication

656 **But if** unless

657 **in his purs** by a fine

658 **helle** an excommunicated person might go to hell for ever. The Summoner thinks a fine a worse punishment

659 **woot ... dede** know that in reality he was lying

660 **Of cursyng ... drede** every guilty man ought to be afraid of excommunication

661 **For curs ... savith** for excommunication will kill, just as absolution will save

662 **And ... *Significavit*** and he [the guilty man]l should also beware of a *Significavit*. (The opening Latin word of a writ, issued by the Archdeacon to the civil authorities, certifying that an excommunicated man had remained obstinate after forty days; the penalty was imprisonment)

663 **daunger** jurisdiction, control

at ... gise to do with as he liked

664 **girles** the young of both sexes

diocise diocese (the area over which a bishop has responsibility)

665 **hir conseil** their secrets

al hir reed their only counsellor

666 **gerland** garland (of leaves and flowers)

667 **greet** large

ale-stake taverns used to advertise themselves by hanging a bush or garland from a pole outside

668 **bokeleer** buckler, shield

cake loaf (held in his lap)

LINES 669–714   The Pardoner

A pardoner sold pardons or indulgences. These were reductions or remissions of the punishment (penance) imposed upon the penitent in the confessional, or of punishment in Purgatory. (They are not the absolution from sin which a priest is empowered to give to a repentant sinner.) Pardons were certificates of remission of penance, which had been introduced in return for gifts to an ecclesiastical charity. The system got out of control and was abused, for example by unlicensed pardoners who sold false relics. The sale of indulgences was the abuse which provoked the Reformation of the sixteenth century. The Pardoner is the last of the pilgrims, and the most corrupt.

Make sure you understand the distinction between pardon and absolution explained above. The portrait is full of false credentials as well as false relics. What is the connection between the Pardoner's false pardons and his lack of masculinity? Why is the Pardoner with the Summoner? (see Characterisation, on Ecclesiastical Villains).

670 **Rouncivale** the hospital of St Mary, Rounceval, near Charing Cross, London. (Rounceval belonged to the Prior of Rouncevall in Navarre)

    compeer fellow, crony

671 **court of Rome** the Pardoner claims to come from the Roman Curia, the source of authorised indulgences

672 **'Com ... to me'** a popular song. The rhyme of 'Rome' and 'to me' confirms that -e was pronounced at the end of a line

673 **bar ... burdoun** accompanied him in a strong bass. (A homosexual relationship may be suggested)

674 **trompe** trumpet

675 **wex** wax

676 **But ... flex** but it hung straight, as does a hank of flax

677 **By ounces ... hadde** the few locks that he had hung separately

678 **And ... overspradde** and he spread them over his shoulders

679 **But ... oon** but the hair lay in single strands

680 **jolitee** prettiness

681 **walet** pouch

682 **Hyme ... jet** it seemed to him that he rode in the latest fashion

683 **Dischevelee, save** with hair unbound, except for

685 **vernycle** Veronica. (After St Veronica, who offered her veil to Christ on the way to Calvary so that he could wipe his face. The veil, with the impression of Christ's face, was kept at St Peter's in Rome. Pilgrims to Rome often wore copies of it)

686 **lappe** large pocket

687 **Bretful** full to the brim

pardun pardons

hoot like cakes freshly made (part of the Pardoner's sales-talk)

688 **smal ... goot** thin as a goat has; that is, unbroken

690 **late** recently

691 **trowe** believe

geldyng a castrated horse. The Pardoner is effeminate

692 **fro ... Ware** from Berwick-on-Tweed to Ware, Hertfordshire. (That is, from the north of England to the south, as these towns are at each end of the Great North Road from Scotland to London)

694 **male** mail bag

pilwe-beer pillowcase

695 **Oure Lady veyl** the veil of Our Lady (the Virgin Mary)

696 **gobet** gobbet, piece

seyl sail

697 **wente** walked

698 **see** sea

hente took up, saved (see Mark 15:7–11)

699 **croys of latoun** crucifix of brass

701 **relikes** relics. Until the 1960s, a Catholic altar had to incorporate a physical relic of a martyr. The cult of relics, a focus of popular piety, was often abused

702 **A povre ... lond** a poor parson living in his country parish

703 **Upon ... moneye** in one day he got for himself more money

704 **tweye** two

705 **feyned** feigned

japes tricks

706 **apes** gulls, fools

707 **trewely to tellen** to be serious

708 **ecclesiaste** the Pardoner was probably not a cleric

709 **lessoun** lesson (a Bible reading)

709 **storie** such as a Saint's Life, or the Pardoner's own moral tale

710 **alderbest** best of all

offertorie anthem sung at the offertory (see line 450)

711 **wiste** knew

712 **preche** preach

affile smooth

714 **murierly** more merrily

LINES 715–24   Recapitulation

715 **clause** short sentence

716 **estaat** condition

719 **Belle** the Bell, another hostelry

720 **to yow ... telle** to tell you

721 **How ... nyght** what we did with ourselves that same night

722 **alyght** alighted, settled

723 **wol** will

viage journey

LINES 725–46   Apology

Chaucer apologises for gross language on the grounds that he is obliged to report the pilgrims' words exactly as they were spoken: a joke which reminds us that the pilgrimage is a fiction. He then apologises for his recent negligence in not having put the pilgrims in order of rank.

In fact he has observed precedence with some care: a joke which draws attention to the form of the fiction.

726 **n'arette** do not impute

vileynye ill-breeding, grossness

728 **cheere** demeanour

729 **Ne ... proprely** not even if I speak their words, with accuracy in each case

730 **al so** as

732 **He moot ... kan** he should repeat, as closely, as he can

733 **Everich** every

charge commission

734 **Al ... large** however rudely and freely he [the man of line 731] speak

735 **untrewe** falsely

736 **feyne thyng** feign things

737 **spare** relent

he the man of line 731

738 **moot as well** must impartially

739 **Crist ... writ** Christ himself spoke very broadly in the Scriptures

740 **woot** know

741 **Eek ... rede** also Plato says, whoever can read him. No-one in England could read Greek, but this idea from the philosopher's *Timaeus* is mentioned in books Chaucer had translated

742 **moote be cosyn** must be cousin

744 **Al** if

degree social rank

746 **My wit is short** I am not sufficiently clever

THE TALE-TELLING GAME (LINES 747–858)

LINES 747–809   The Host's proposal

The Host is as important to the *Tales* as any pilgrim, since he referees the tale-telling game. Later, the Cook calls him Harry Bailly; an innkeeper of this name is mentioned in the records for Southwark at this period.

Why does the Host make this proposal?

Does his speech give a clue to his character? (see The Road to Canterbury).

747 **Greet ... everichon** our host entertained us all very well

748 **soper** supper (a communal meal)

750 **leste** it pleased

751 **semely** suitable

HOOSTE Host, innkeeper

withalle moreover, too

752 **For ... halle** [fit] to have been a marshal [master of ceremonies] in a hall

753 **stepe** prominent

754 **Chepe** Cheapside, the market of the City of London. As Southwark was less respectable than the City, this is a compliment to the Host

755 **ytaught** instructed [in his trade]

756 **And ... naught** he was in no way lacking in manhood

758 **pleyen** to play, jest

760 **maad our rekenynges** paid our bills

761 **lordynges** my masters [used like 'Ladies and Gentlemen']

762 **Ye ... hertely** you are indeed heartily welcome to my house

764 **saugh nat** have not seen

765 **Atones** at one time

herberwe harbour, inn

766 **Fayn ... how** I would dearly like to entertain you, if I knew how

767 **bythoght** struck by a thought

769 **God yow speede** may God bring you success

770 **The blisful ... meede!** May the blessed martyr [St Thomas] bring you your reward

771 **wel I woot** as I well know

by the weye along the road

772 **Ye ... pleye** You intend to tell stories and amuse yourselves

773 **is noon** there is no

775 **maken yow disport** devise entertainment for you

776 **erst** first

777 **yow liketh** it pleases you

778 **stonden at** stand by, accept

779 **werken** do

781 **Now ... deed** Now by the soul of my father, who is dead

782 **But ... heed!** if you do not enjoy it, you can strike off my head

783 **Hoold ... hondes** in sign of agreement

784 **Oure ... seche** it did not take long to discover our opinion

785 **Us ... wys** we did not think it was worth while to deliberate seriously

786 **avys** consideration

787 **voirdit ... leste** whatever decision he pleased

788 **quod** said

herkneth ... beste listen carefully

789 **But ... desdeyn** but do not treat it with disdain, I beg you

791 **to ... weye** so to shorten our journey

792 **tweye** two

793 **To ... so** I mean, on the way to Canterbury

794 **And ... two** and he shall tell another two on the way home

795 **Of ... bifalle** of adventures that have happened in the past

796 **which** the one

796 **bereth hym** manages
797 **in this caas** on this occasion
798 **sentence** meaning, significance
   solaas solace, comfort
799 **oure aller cost** the expense of the rest of us
801 **agayn** back
804 **Right ... cost** at my own expense
   gyde guide
805 **And ... withseye** whoever shall dispute my judgement
806 **paye al** pay for all
807 **vouche sauf** grant
808 **anon ... mo** immediately, without further discussion
809 **erly ... therefore** get ready for the journey early

LINES 810–21   The tale-telling game: the pilgrims' acceptance

Why do the pilgrims accept? What effect does it have on the pilgrimage (see The Road to Canterbury)?

810 **and ... swore** and our oaths were sworn
813 **governour** president
814 **juge and reportour** judge and reporter
815 **And ... pris** and arrange a supper at a set price
816 **reuled been** be ruled
   at his devys at his pleasure
817 **In ... assent** in great things and small; and so, unanimously
819 **fet anon** fetched immediately
820 **echon** each of us

LINES 822–58   The tale-telling game: the setting-forth and the cut

What is the implication of lines 835–41? What is the effect of line 844 (see The Road to Canterbury)?

822 **Amorwe** in the morning
823 **cok** cock, the male bird who leads the hens out
825 **riden ... paas** rode at little more than a walking pace
826 **Wateryng ... Thomas** a stream where pilgrims watered their horses near the second milestone on the Canterbury road

827 **bigan ... arest** pulled his horse up

828 **leste** please

829 **Ye ... recorde** you know your promise, and I remind you of it

830 **If ... accorde** if evening-song and morning-song agree. (If you have not changed your tune)

832 **As ... ale** as I hope never to drink anything but wine or ale

835 **draweth** take. A polite plural imperative addressed to the more gentle pilgrims

cut lots (Different lengths, perhaps of straw, are to be drawn from the Host's hand to decide who tells the first tale. The Host doubtless arranges that the Knight should draw the short straw)

ferrer twynne depart further (from the inn)

838 **accord** decision

840 **lat ... shamefastnesse** leave aside your modesty

841 **Ne ... man!** stop dreaming: put out your hand and take your straw, everyone

842 **wight** man

844 **Were ... cas** either by luck, or fate, or chance

845 **sothe** sooth, truth

fil fell

847 **And ... resoun** and tell his tale he must, as was reasonable

848 **foreward** agreement

composicioun agreement

849 **han herd** have heard

what ... mo more needs to be said?

851 **As he that** as a man who

853 **Syn** since

854 **a** by

855 **herkneth** listen!

857 **cheere** manner

PART THREE

CRITICAL APPROACHES

LITERARY GENRES AND MODES

The General Prologue draws on several different genres or kinds of writing. It is a prologue in which the author speaks to his audience, introducing a larger work. A medieval prologue aimed to capture the good will of its auditors and readers, to lay out what is to follow, and to apologise for any inadequacies. This prologue consists of a formal opening (lines 1–18); the introduction of the pilgrimage and of the narrator (lines 19–41); a catalogue of portraits of his companions (lines 42–714); the apology (lines 725–46); the setting-up of the tale-telling game (lines 747–821); the riding out, and the drawing of lots for who shall tell the first tale (lines 822–58).

The catalogue of portraits takes up almost four-fifths of the Prologue. Detailed description can become static, and catalogues can become repetitious. But Chaucer varies his approach and is unpredictable. His prologue is also a narrative: each pilgrim is described not only in terms of his or her profession, appearance and character but also in terms of how they strike their fellow-pilgrim, Chaucer. He half dramatises many of them, conveying the impression that they have spoken to him and that he is passing on what they say. This relationship between the narrator and his creations keeps the descriptions alive. The narrative quickens in the final section as the Host chivvies and persuades the pilgrims, leads them out of Southwark, and arranges the cut so that the Knight should tell the first tale.

As well as prologue, description and narrative, the General Prologue also draws on the materials of **satire**. Satire is the holding up to ridicule of folly and vice, and medieval satire attacked its victims harshly. Satire of the three estates of medieval society caricatured the typical faults of the members of the military, clerical and lay estates, as in *Piers Plowman*, which has a hunting monk, a flattering friar and some venal laymen who also appear in Chaucer. But Chaucer uses a different approach, partly drawn from the thirteenth-century French *Roman de la Rose,* an encyclopaedic narrative work, the beginning of which he had translated as *The Romaunt of the Rose*. The French poem is a **dream-vision**, in which a dreamer meets and describes various personages, who talk and interact with him. The *Roman* does not attack the targets of its satire but allows them to speak. Chaucer does likewise, and he develops a technique of **ironical** praise, examined below. Thus the Prologue uses a number of genres, modes and approaches. It is not a work of naïve realism or of straightforward social observation, although it contains elements which allow modern readers accustomed to realism to read much of it in that way.

Something must be said of the work which the Prologue introduces. *The Canterbury Tales* is a very varied miscellany of tales such as might be told by a mixed group of pilgrims on the road to Canterbury. The work is united by the framework of the tale-telling competition, and though the pilgrims do not even reach Canterbury, the pattern is clear. At its simplest it is a compilation of various stories set inside two **frame-stories**, the pilgrimage and the tale-telling game. The Prologue sets up the game, and it also sets up the human skittles at the beginning of its own game. The Host's game nearly comes to a halt as soon as the Knight finishes the first tale. The Host's authority is flouted by the drunken Miller, who insults him and the Knight and the Reeve. Pilgrims quarrel and fall out of charity. The Knight later stops the Host attacking the Pardoner. Chaucer's tale is stopped by the Host. Some pilgrims do not speak, others talk a lot, notably the Wife of Bath. Tales are interrupted or stopped by the Host or other pilgrims. A runaway servant rides up and joins the pilgrimage. Finally the Cook falls off his horse, and the Parson tells the last tale. The frame-story is social comedy, not without a hint of the more serious purpose of a pilgrimage. Some tales are very serious indeed.

The General Prologue is an expository introduction and overture to the *Tales*, hinting at some of the themes as well as introducing the tellers of the tales. Because it is varied and self-contained, and as vivid as medieval manuscript illuminations, it is often read on its own. Thus detached, it becomes a picture of the society of the time, especially as the gallery of portraits of the pilgrims is a cross-section of those who were free to go on a pilgrimage. It is also written in a lively and realistic style, so that we can imagine that Chaucer did meet actual people resembling his fellow-pilgrims. Chaucer's story-telling art allows us to combine with the interest of understanding something of medieval society the pleasure of becoming involved with a 'real' set of people.

The Prologue was, however, intended as a prologue, something 'spoken before'. Chaucer probably read it aloud to friends and at court, and wrote it so that we should imagine him doing so. Audiences who knew Chaucer would have enjoyed the idea of his accidentally falling in with a ready-made group of pilgrims and of their fictional adventures. They would have certainly been amused at the figure Chaucer cuts later on in the *Tales*. The Host addresses him as a fat little man, too shy to tell a story. When pressed, the pilgrim Chaucer begins on a feeble romance, a **parody** of bad popular romances: it rhymes so wretchedly that the Host cannot endure it and rudely prevents his own author from continuing. Like the original audience, we know that this supposedly autobiographical story is not true. Chaucer may have gone on such a pilgrimage, but it is not likely that its members spoke in verse, nor that their tales would have been audible from horseback. The appearance of **verisimilitude** is brilliant and at times intense, but it is a deliberate illusion. Chaucer often dispenses with this verisimilitude: many of the tales are fantastic, whether adventurous, miraculous, indecent or farcical. Some tales are doctrinal; the Parson's is not a story but a treatise on penance. The verisimilitude of the Prologue is only one of his literary modes.

Chaucer has an eye for social realities, but it would not have occurred to him to write social history or a naturalistic novel. The pilgrims were dreamed up because the tales which are to follow had to have tellers to tell them. On examination, each of the portraits proves to be formal and self-contained, as they are not in novels. Also each pilgrim belongs to a different profession, except for the Second Nun and five Guildsmen. This suggests that Chaucer meant to show a representative cross-section of society, as in estates satire, in which the faults of the three estates were held up for correction. He includes only those who were likely to go on such a pilgrimage. Pilgrimages would not include serfs or poor peasants not free to travel. A nobleman would travel with his own retinue. Thus the base and apex of the feudal pyramid are not here. There are twenty-six men and three women: women would normally stay at home unless, like the Prioress and her opposite number the Wife of Bath, they were independent.

Chaucer could not guess that readers six centuries later would think of him and his pilgrims as typically medieval. His purposes differed from those of, for example, George Eliot, who certainly meant the characters of her novel *Middlemarch* (published in 1872) to represent the historical life of a Midlands town in the early nineteenth century. So long as we bear this difference in mind, there is no harm in seeing the pilgrims as English men and women of the later Middle Ages. They are presented as typical human beings, and have social and economic as well as moral and spiritual dimensions. Many of them are types who would have been familiar to lettered and unlettered people in the audience: the hunting monk, the venal friar, the dedicated knight, the gay young squire, the ladylike prioress, the good parson. All these were figures known to popular as well as literary tradition, as caricatures or as ideals. The central figure of the slightly earlier poem *Piers Plowman* is an idealised ploughman, like Chaucer's ploughman.

The portraits belong in the Prologue as part of a developing fictional action. To use a theatrical analogy, it is as if *The Canterbury Tales* were a play which opened with the cast assembled on the stage at the beginning instead of at the end. A true historical sense involves us in seeing these characters as living: when we see the Merchant, we see a pompous businessman, not just a typical representative of an emerging class in the City of London in the late fourteenth century. Later on he turns out to be unhappily married, and becomes a typical human being as well as a typical merchant.

CHAUCER AND NARRATIVE

The Prologue is unusual in that its narrator is also a character in his own fiction. The author acts as reporter. After the initial description of spring, we hear (lines 30–2) how Chaucer made himself one of the pilgrims:

> And shortly, whan the sonne was to reste,
> So hadde I spoken with hem everichon
> That I was of hir felaweshipe anon … (lines 30–2)

We gather that Chaucer was a sociable pilgrim; his previous comments on the accommodation at the Tabard indicate that he appreciated its amenity and enjoyed company. (People travelled the roads in companies for security reasons; some of the pilgrims were armed. Chaucer was robbed two or three times.) Chaucer tells us that he had a 'ful devout corage' (line 22), but medieval religion did not stop him enjoying convivial company. The modesty with which he offers to describe his companions confirms him as affable and unaffected.

But we know quite a lot about this disarming fellow, and his audience knew more, for he had written many poems in which he presents himself in a similar way. He was an experienced king's man, a diplomat, an MP, a JP, a retired customs officer. It was his job to win people's confidence, to get them talking. He knew his fellow men and the tricks they get up to. The original audience knew things about Chaucer that we cannot know – especially if they had seen and heard him read his works. But thanks to scholars and to a reading of his earlier works, we can be sure that his previous reputation played a part in the reception of the tale he is now beginning.

He says in lines 35–42 that he thinks it reasonable, before he goes any further in his tale, to tell us the condition, occupation, rank and dress of each of his companions. The military estate is described without any obvious **irony**. But we do not have to read very far into the description of the Prioress (lines 118–62) to realise that, however uncomplicated and impressionable Chaucer the pilgrim may pretend to be, he conveys things about the other pilgrims that seem to be beyond the easy-going fellow who made himself a member of their company. Chaucer the pilgrim seems to be very impressed by the Prioress's ladylike manners, yet makes us aware that her charity is directed toward her dogs. Love, for the Prioress, conquers all (line 162), and Chaucer too seems to be under the influence. At the outset of the portrait of the Monk, our suspicions are further aroused. We are told that the Monk was 'a manly man, to been an abbot able'. The idea that manliness qualifies a monk to be an abbot is comic, since monks are vowed to celibacy. A standard contemporary joke against monks. But could it also be a joke at the expense of the simplicity of the speaker, the pilgrim named Chaucer? Or at anyone who entertains the notion that the qualification for becoming abbot is a commandingly masculine appearance? Immediately afterwards we hear that the bells on the Monk's bridle rang 'als cleere / And eek as loude as dooth the chapel belle' (line 171). We already know that the Monk (who is vowed to poverty) has many horses and is fond of hunting (monastic estates offered plenty of land to hunt over). This last line insinuates, once again in a slyly comic way, that the Monk obeyed the summons of the hunt more promptly than that of the chapel. Is the pilgrim narrator unconscious of this irony, and the straightfaced poet enjoying a little joke? This variable perspective haunts the Prologue.

The pleasant sociability of the pilgrim Chaucer may well have been part of his creator's own character: social ease is part of the diplomat's life. Chaucer's disciple, the fifteenth-century poet John Lydgate, testified that Chaucer 'seyde alwey the beste'. Yet retired customs officers, however agreeable, are not impressionable. We sense a play between the narrator and the poet. Is the man in the poem the same as the man who wrote the poem and read it to his audiences? This question was first put and answered (negatively) by E.T. Donaldson in his *Speaking of Chaucer*, 1970, but it has been sensed by all who have enjoyed what the American poet Ezra Pound called 'the Chaucerian chuckle'. It follows that we do not always accept what the speaker says about the other pilgrims, nearly all of whom seem to impress him hugely, with the exception of the low-class rogues who bring up the rear. The gallery of portraits is thus viewed from two angles simultaneously – the social surface of every character, as disclosed to the narrator's innocent eye, but with something of each pilgrim's inner nature also, disclosed by the poet.

Another way of taking this is not to separate Chaucer-the-pilgrim from Chaucer-the-poet, but to regard it all as part of his irony. Irony is a rhetorical technique, critical discussions of which can become very complicated. But it is a speech-habit common in everyday life. Essentially, it means saying one thing while conveying another. Thus, some of the many pilgrims Chaucer calls 'worthy' seem entirely unworthy (the Friar, for example). Among those whom he calls good fellows are the Shipman, a thief, and the Summoner, a corrupt officer of the church court. A more complex instance of irony is when Chaucer tells us in line 183 that he *said* that the Monk's opinion was good. The Monk has just given it as his opinion that holy men may hunt, and that a monk need not stay in his cloister. But Benedictine monks take a vow of stability: to stay in the monastery to praise God in the liturgy and the monastic office of prayer, rather than rolling about the world.

The Rule of St Benedict also enjoins study and manual labour, and the renunciation of the world and of personal possessions – such as a stable of fine horses. It is clear that the Monk does not observe the Benedictine Rule, and strains even a relaxed observance of that Rule. It is clear too that the reader is to notice this contradiction. To the original audience, the hunting Monk was a familiar figure of **satire**: a well-mounted gentleman in a well-filled habit, who once strayed into the cloister and has now strayed out of it: a rubicund renouncer of this world, riding in the medieval equivalent of a Rolls-Royce and enjoying it.

But Chaucer does not denounce the Monk. On the contrary, he praises him, agrees with him, admires his splendid horse, boots, physique, taste and diet. Irony relies for its success on the knowledge and alertness of the audience. This is more reliable when the author reads his poem facing his audience than when his written text is read silently by readers remote in time or place. Some critics think that the play of Chaucer's irony, habitual even in his early writings, is not well served by drawing a hard and fast distinction between the pilgrim Chaucer and the poet Chaucer. They prefer that we should imagine ourselves in the original audiences who listened to Chaucer, knowing him and knowing that he was by no means the impressionable person or **persona** he presents in the Prologue. They prefer to describe the effect of these disparities between what is said and what is meant as irony. We certainly should compare Chaucer's expressed opinions with what he tells us elsewhere in a portrait. Whether we talk about pilgrim and poet, or whether we talk about irony, makes little difference. But it is essential not to take everything Chaucer says simply at face value.

It should be recognised that a naïve or gullible narrator is common in fiction – as in Swift's *Gulliver's Travels* (1726). It was especially common in the **dream-vision** poems so prominent in the narrative literature of the thirteenth and fourteenth centuries. Two of the poems Chaucer imitated, the French *Romance of the Rose* and Dante's *Divine Comedy*, were dream-visions in which the dreamer is ignorant and has to be instructed by the figures he meets in his dream, and particularly by his guide. Three of the greatest English poems of Chaucer's day were dream-visions also: Langland's *Piers Plowman*, Gower's *Confessio Amantis* and the anonymous *Pearl*. Chaucer translated the *Roman de la Rose*. Except for *Troilus and Criseyde* all his longer poems before the *Tales* are dream-visions. Chaucer often makes himself a comic figure in these early poems, and is always having a joke with the audience in a way often thought to be characteristically English. There was, then, nothing surprising in the idea of Chaucer asking us to laugh at him as well as with him. In the language of the comic stage, Chaucer the pilgrim is the 'straight man' who allows the people he meets to do all the talking – and to give themselves away in the process.

A frequent feature of the dream-vision was that the dreamer met at the outset a number of personified abstractions whose portraits are given in series. That is how the *Romance of the Rose* begins, and J.V. Cunningham pointed out that the General Prologue adapts this useful expository device into a more realistic mode. (J.V. Cunningham. 'Convention as Structure – The Prologue to *The Canterbury Tales*' in *Geoffrey Chaucer: A Critical Anthology*, edited by J.A. Burrow, Penguin Books, Harmondsworth, 1969, pp. 218–32.) Chaucer's adaptation has been so successful that the origins of this device of the dreamer in the portrait-gallery have been forgotten.

The final section of the Prologue, in which the pilgrims accept the Host's proposal of a tale-telling game, in which he is to be the judge, is also illuminated by this parallel with the dream-vision. The Host becomes the pilgrims' guide, and all the pilgrims agree to obey him. Like the guides in Chaucer's early poems, the Host is a manipulator – talkative, uncontrollable and slightly mischievous. As master of the game, he is not altogether a suitable figure to preside over a pilgrimage: he drinks and swears, and teases and bullies the less important pilgrims, notably Chaucer himself. Rather like Falstaff at the end of Shakespeare's *Henry IV*, he overdoes things, and has to be snubbed at the end; in this case by the Parson. A richly comic character, the Host plays many roles in the pilgrimage.

Contemporary audiences, however, would have noticed that the innocent narrator's confidence was easily won by the Host, and would also have been familiar with stories where a rash promise (such as all the pilgrims make to obey the Host) turns out alarmingly. The Host is a jolly character, and has often been seen as the incarnation of a Merrie England unreformed by the puritan Reformation. He does indeed turn the pilgrimage into a merry game, a rather mad game, but by the same token we must expect such a figure to be dethroned at the end – as the Lord of Misrule was in medieval comic plays. Indeed the Pardoner, an expert on drinking, describes the tavern as the devil's temple. But he was sitting in a pub at the time, and is later exposed as a fake by the Host himself. It would be a grave mistake to see the Host as a figure of the Devil – after all, Chaucer's family had made their living by selling drink – but it would also be a mistake to take him, or any of the pilgrims, as Chaucer the pilgrim does, entirely at their face value.

Finally, to complete Chaucer's humorous presentation of himself, we should know of his later appearance in *The Canterbury Tales*. The Host calls upon Chaucer to tell a tale,

> And seyde thus: 'What man artow?' quod he;
> 'Thou lookest as thou woldest fynde an hare,
> For evere upon the ground I se thee stare.
>
> Approche neer, and looke up murily.
> Now war yow, sires, and lat this man have place.
> He in the waast is shape as wel as I …

artow art thou
quod said
woldest wouldst
war yow pay attention
waast waist

The Host, who is stout, is having a joke at Chaucer's girth.

> This were a popet in an arm t'enbrace
> For any womman, smal and fair of face.
> He semeth elvyssh by his contenaunce,
> For unto no wight dooth he daliaunce.

popet doll
t'enbrace to embrace
smal slender
fair attractive
elvyssh elflike
contenaunce look
For … daliaunce he pays court to no man

Chaucer has hardly begun his tale of Sir Thopas when the Host stops him with extreme rudeness. Chaucer punishes this bumptious creature by telling another tale, about Melibee, a long moral **allegory** stuffed with wise sentences and maxims.

CHARACTERISATION

Chaucer's characterisation in the General Prologue is celebrated. But before we look at the portraits, we should notice their order. Beforehand, Chaucer says (lines 30–42) that he will tell us about the state, profession, rank and appearance of each of the pilgrims, but afterwards apologises for his informality: 'Also I prey yow to foryeve it me, / Al have I nat set folk in hir degree' (lines 743–4). This apology draws attention to the order, and turns out to be partly a joke, for he has in fact set folk in their degree, according to a hierarchy both social and moral: the good Knight at the top and the fraudulent Pardoner at the bottom. It is true that the final bunch of pilgrims, the rogues, seem to have been tagged on (line 541) almost as an afterthought. But in general Chaucer has observed the rule of precedence which the social hierarchy dictated. Feudal precedence was being challenged by the power of new money, and by the numbers of men leaving the manor after the Black Death.

THE ESTATES

The military estate is followed by the clerical estate; the clerics by the laity; an upper-middle class by a lower-middle class; with the rascals at the end. Further, within this apparently casual order of descending importance and merit, there is an order created by contrasts in juxtaposition: the Knight fights for his lord, the Squire for his lady; the Merchant talks of his prospering business, the Clerk of moral virtue; the Clerk's cope is threadbare, the Friar's is new. On inspection, the catalogue is found to have moral patterns. It is not, as Chaucer pretends, a set of notes on some striking individuals, nor a social cross-section of interest to historians.

    The order of appearance goes like this (with the number of lines in each portrait given in brackets):

THE ESTATES continued

(1) Military estate:	Knight (35 lines), Squire (21), Yeoman (16): 72 in all
(2) Clerical estate:	Prioress (44), Monk (43), Friar (61): 148
(3) Professionals:	Merchant (14), Clerk (23), Sergeant of the Law (21), Franklin (29), Guildsmen (18) and Cook (8): 113
(4) Good Men:	Parson (51), Ploughman (12): 63
(5) Stewards:	Miller (21), Manciple (19), Reeve (35): 75
(6) Church Officers:	Summoner (45), Pardoner (45): 90

Medieval social theory divided the king's subjects into three estates: the Military, the Clergy and the Laity. Chaucer observes this division, although the Clerk and Parson, a member of the secular clergy, are included with the Laity. The Laity – groups 3, half of 4, and 5 – are arranged in only a rough order of precedence, unlike the first two estates. The Sergeant of the Law, for example, would outrank the two men introduced before him, and the Franklin, as an established landholder, would outrank the newly rich Sergeant. These minor departures from precedence make the catalogue seem more impromptu, casual and informal. The Laity are divided into three groups here: the financially independent professionals, and those who work for them; with, between the two, the Parson and Ploughman, men poor in the things of this world but free from hypocrisy and avarice. Finally, we have the ecclesiastical villains.

The clerical estate gets twice as many lines as the military one, reflecting the volume of anti-clerical satire. The portraits of the Summoner and the Pardoner are also lengthy. As for the third estate, it is noticeable that everyone in groups 3, 5 and 6 is on the make. The only clear exception is the Clerk, who stands in stark contrast between the Merchant and the Sergeant. The Military are exempt from the bourgeois vice of greed, and so are the senior Clergy except for the Friar, though the Monk and the Prioress are a very comfortable lord and lady.

THE MILITARY

Knights had dominated English society since the Norman Conquest, and Chaucer begins his catalogue with a shining example of Christian chivalry, setting an ideal standard, of which nearly all the other pilgrims fall short.

THE KNIGHT

The Knight is defined in terms of his virtues (lines 45–6) and actions to defend the faith, far more than by his appearance and words. The Knight is also distinguished from his son, who has fought against fellow-Christians in France, whereas the Knight's motive is religious. In his courtesy to all and his modest dress he completes the figure of the off-duty soldier as Christian gentleman, and is one of three pilgrims who are presented as admirable. Like the Parson and the Ploughman, the worthy Knight is the ideal of his estate.

All the pilgrims are superlative: each is the perfect example of his or her type and/or profession. The Knight is the antique pattern of the chivalry of Edward III's time.

THE SQUIRE

The Squire is a type of gallant young lover, fresh and fashionable, perhaps like some in the court audience. His description is an example of the principle of contrast which governs much of the arrangement of the Prologue, even down to apparently casual detail. The Knight had good horses but was not gay in appearance himself (line 74); indeed his coarse tunic is all rusty. His son dresses like a picture of the spring; he cuts a fine figure on a horse (line 94), but no horse is mentioned. The father fights in his lord's war, and has thrice slain his foe; for his part, the son has done well for a beginner in his *chyvachie* across the Channel, in the hope of gaining his lady's favour. (Chaucer himself had been a French prisoner-of-war by the time he was twenty; the Black Prince, Edward III's son and Richard II's father, had led the English army into battle at the age of fifteen.) The Squire's prowess is that of a lover: like the birds of lines 9–11, he does not sleep at night. If he is treated with some amusement, the Squire is harmless; Chaucer's attitude seems indulgent rather than censorious, not unlike that of Duke Theseus in the Knight's Tale towards the young lovers Palamon and Arcite: Theseus remembers that he was a lover himself when young. And the Squire is a dutiful son.

THE YEOMAN

The Yeoman's portrait is vividly pictorial, but anonymous. In keeping with medieval admiration for professional skill, the adverb Chaucer chooses to describe the way the Yeoman looked after his *takel* is 'yeomanlike'. He is every inch an archer and a forester, resplendent in the badges of his trade. The archers in the English army were instrumental in winning the battles of the Hundred Years War (1337–1453). The Knight and his follower are thus an emblem of the great English past; the Squire, between them, is an example of a fashionable young gentleman.

THE CLERGY

The clerical estate presents a much less worthy trio. The Prioress is a lady to her fingertips; the Monk 'was a lord ful fat and in good poynt'. The Friar is a libertine, a playboy and a confidence trickster. They are not what they should be.

THE PRIORESS

The Prioress's faults are, however, minor. Like most Prioresses in the Middle Ages, she has the manners of the upper class, which the narrator appears to admire greatly, describing them at length. He is also fascinated by her delicious appearance, which is that of a heroine of romance, as is her name. Her tenderness to her dogs, and the ambiguous motto on her rosary, suggest some diversion of interest on the part of one who has dedicated herself as a bride of Christ. Her tale turns out to be as conventionally pious as her manners are fine. The narrator is taken by her refinement and femininity and the appearance of a romantic sensibility. The sustained ambiguity of her portrait is examined in Textual Analysis, Text 2.

THE MONK AND THE FRIAR

Luxury has also affected the other two celibates, the manly Monk and the wanton Friar. The Monk, whose name is later given as Don John, and Friar Huberd both have love tokens, like Madame Eglentyne. The Monk's gold pin with a love-knot (lines 196–7) matches the Nun's gold brooch; the Friar carries a stock of pins to give to pretty women (line 234). Those in religious orders should be self-disciplined but all three regular clergy have personal names (unlike the military trio) and all three have love-tokens: an example of the use of significant detail to link portraits. Both men have luxurious tastes and dress expensively. The Friar's corruption, however, goes deeper than the Monk's.

Monks and nuns had been established in the Church for 1,000 years, and their shortcomings, amusingly displayed here, are those of a worldliness and weakness that was familiar to the laity. Senior monks and nuns were commonly the younger brothers and sisters of the lords and ladies they often resembled. The Friars, however, were only two-and-a-half centuries old, and their hypocrisy was resented, as is clear from the amount of satire they attracted. With a roving commission to beg, they could pry into every household and get the better of the housewife. The Friar's portrait is longer by ten lines than that of any other pilgrim.

The hunting Monk is a familiar caricature and the details of his fine horses, his fur cuffs and his preference for roast swan could be paralleled from other anti-clerical satire in the Middle Ages. It might be more profitable, then, to focus on details of Chaucer's art rather than on his social criticism. Three techniques used in the portrait are repeated elsewhere. Few of the pilgrims are presented entirely by listing visual details, as in the case of the Yeoman; the chief method, especially in satirical portraits, is to describe with admiration and enthusiasm all those features of which the victim himself is particularly proud. Thus the Monk's manliness, fine horses, supple boots and diet are remarked on with warm approval. Secondly, the narrator appears to report or echo the words of the pilgrim's most revealing statements. Thus, lines 174–89 virtually report a conversation in which the Monk gives himself away by protesting against the strictness of the old Rule of St Benedict, although as a Regular, he has bound himself to keep these Rules by a religious vow. However, the pilgrim Chaucer draws further attention to the Monk's laxity by mentioning two other monastic obligations, namely, daily study and manual labour, and crowns the irony by asking how *the world* shall be served. While the established monastic orders provided excellent administrators in secular fields, this was not the intention of their founders, who withdrew from this world in order to prepare for the next. By accepting the Monk's secular role and, in his eagerness to agree, emphasising its (entirely false) premise, Chaucer or his narrator feigns ignorance and creates irony at the extent of the Monk's self-deception or self-forgetfulness.

These two techniques, praising the subject's most inappropriate vices and quoting his idiocies with approval, are part of Chaucer's basic satirical method, which is to allow fools to give themselves away. A third aspect – word-play – is different and elusive, as it relies on an awareness both of historical English and of social history. At line 199 the narrator says the Monk's bald head and jolly face gleamed with good living 'as it had been enoynt'. The monk's head was bald since it had been tonsured in sign of renunciation of manly vanity, and (if he is a priest) had been anointed, not with fat living but with the sacramental oil of Holy Orders. There are still public houses called the Monk's Head, with floridly painted inn signs. The satire is not bitter but comical, as the Monk seems to have a stronger idea of what the monastic ideal is not rather than what it is.

The same ironies are applied more sarcastically to the Friar. He is the most skilful seducer in all the four (celibate) orders (line 211). He kindly arranges marriages – for girls whom he has made pregnant (lines 212–4). He gives an easy penance – in return for a good bribe (lines 223–4). These are examples of vice being praised. Lines 225–30 exemplify the second technique of echoing the Friar's transparent excuses. His plausible patter is again quoted in lines 243–8. There seems to be an obscene *double-entendre* on the word *post* in line 214.

Two further, more poetic, features are exemplified in the portrait of the Friar. One is the use of the rhyming couplet for the purposes of comic anticlimax, as in:

> Ful wel biloved and famulier was he
> With frankeleyns over all in his contree. (lines 215–16)

The first line praises the Friar's gift of friendly intimacy and raises expectations that the object of this brotherly attention will be the deserving poor. The second reveals that he prefers the society of people who can entertain him luxuriously. In lines 223–4, the rhyme *penaunce/pitaunce* is particularly telling. Finally, there is a rare example of a poetic simile:

> And in his harpyng, when that he hadde songe
> His eyen twynkled in his heed aryght
> As doon the sterres in the frosty nyght. (lines 265–7)

Most of the images in the Prologue are proverbial; this is more decorative. However, the comparison of the charming Friar's twinkling eyes to the stars is rendered suddenly chilling by the inclusion of *frosty*.

The calculating nature of the professional parasite is delicately revealed. It is by these tiny touches that the poet makes his effects, and converts the stereotypes of satire into recognisable people. It is because he speaks of them so sympathetically and admiringly for being what they are, that Chaucer is often regarded as being a humorous and comic writer rather than a reforming satirist.

PROFESSIONALS

THE MERCHANT
After the lavishness of the Friar's description, the Merchant's is short and understated. Yet every seemingly off-hand line tells us more about this man of substance: four on his good clothes; four on his talk, boastful and fearful by turns; five on his shady financial dealing; an inconclusive final couplet.

Chaucer's pretended guilelessness is now so well established that we expect him to be impressed by anyone. He prattles on, full of empty phrases like 'ful well', 'for anything', 'For sothe'. In the last couplet he reinforces 'for sothe' with 'sooth to sey', and artlessly repeats 'worthy man' from line 279. We remember that Chaucer, according to Lydgate, 'seyde alwey the beste'. Yet the poet conveys to us that even his social **persona** finds the Merchant rather hard work: he was worthy (that is, he seemed a sound man) but chose not to give his name. The Merchant may have travelled in company for safety's sake. His self-importance about his business is self-defeating, since his confidential remark to the narrator that no-one knew he was in debt (line 280) is gossiped to the whole world. We now appreciate the force of lines 31–2: 'So hadde I spoken with hem everichon / That I was of hir felaweship anon.'

THE CLERK
The Clerk is a contrast to the Merchant, as the Squire was to the Knight. The Merchant is worldly, the Clerk unworldly, and this shows in every detail of their clothes, mounts, interests and conversation. The man of money booms his business; the philosopher is crisp and instructive. The portraits are linked by the word *sownynge* (lines 275, 307). Chaucer's man-of-the-world persona is amused by the Clerk's unworldliness, and jokes about this philosopher who has no gold. But the writer speaks

warmly about the Clerk's love of books, his true piety and his elevated, economical speech. The difference between the poet's values and those of his social persona is evident.

THE SERGEANT OF THE LAW

The Sergeant is another impressively learned man, but with plenty of gold in his coffer. He applies his skills to personal enrichment, in further contrast to the Oxford cleric. It can be seen now that the placing of the Clerk's portrait was for dramatic and moral contrast, not for social precedence. The theme of greed is forced into prominence by this sandwiching of the spiritual man between the men of substance. (The lawyer may be the more substantial, since he turns his fees and robes into land.)

The manner and conversation of the three men are again compared. The lawyer's words seemed worthy of reverence (lines 312–3), whereas the Clerk's few words were spoken with reverence. The Clerk's wisdom is seen in the 'hy sentence' and 'moral virtue' of his speech; the Sergeant's words seemed wise, but his expertise has brought him wariness and discretion – canny prudence rather than wisdom. His *writyng* (line 326) was more reliable than his word, for writing secured title to land. A distrust of lawyers shows in the use of the word *semed* (line 322) repeated from line 313. The simplicity of line 322 makes it as effective today as it was 500 years ago, despite all the changes in the language.

THE FRANKLIN

The companion of the purchaser of land is a land-holder. The Franklin's assured social standing exempts him from the moneymaking that affects other pilgrims, but in his Epicureanism (see below – The Doctor of Physic) he shows the same gusto in self-gratification that makes even the most wayward pilgrim so enjoyable. The Franklin's philosophy and style of life are picturesquely described, with poetic figures (lines 332, 345–6, 358); the final lines list the important offices that had brought him into contact with the Sergeant.

The picture of country hospitality is the first of many in English, done with a Chaucerian combination of cordiality, freshness, slight hyperbole and affectionate mockery, as in:

> Ful many a fat partrich hadde he in muwe,
> And many a breem and many a luce in stuwe. (lines 349–50)

As often in Chaucer, it is at the rhyme that the wit becomes apparent:

> Whit was his berd as is a dayesye.
> Of his complexioun he was sangwyn.
> Wel loved he by the morwe a sop in wyn. (lines 332–4)

The simple, factual lines succeed each other without a hint of malice, yet the rhyming of *sangwyn* with *wyn* suggests that the wine may have helped the blood in producing the Franklin's ruddy complexion. This kind of identical rhyme was admired. The good living of the Franklin is not regarded critically, if one can go by the innocence of the comparisons to the daisy and morning milk.

THE GUILDSMEN

The absence of a link between the Franklin and the Guildsmen contributes to the unpremeditated air of Chaucer's report on his fellow pilgrims. The Guildsmen are perhaps the least interesting members of the pilgrimage, partly because they are not individualised (none of them tells a tale), partly because they are the object of a satire that is rather predictable. The guilds, though their members were artisans, were wealthy enough to ignore the sumptuary laws. Sumptuary law prescribed the particular type of dress which was to be worn by each class and trade (see note to line 366). Aldermen, and more especially their wives, have been an easy target for satire ever since the Middle Ages. Their simple pride in their wealth and their wives' social pretensions amuse Chaucer – as is shown in the superb **hyperbole** of *roialliche* in the last line, an example of the poet's intuitive understanding of the social fantasies of the worthy matrons. Another irony is the approval given by the narrator to this social pride in externals and status in line 375.

THE COOK

The Guildsmen have their own cook, a sign of affluence and pretension. Like all the pilgrims, the Cook is the best of his kind, and Chaucer delights as usual in giving us all the special language of this particular art. But despite the narrator's enthusiasm, his dishes sound ordinary enough, compared with the fare expected of the Franklin's cook. Is the *mormal* on his shin the result of his connoisseurship of London's ale? This is the sort of question prompted by the straightfaced (repulsive) juxtaposition of the *mormal* and *blankmanger*. As with the Franklin's *sangwyn* complexion, we cannot be sure, but that Chaucer enjoyed such urbane ironies is certain. His background would also have given him a thorough knowledge of the catering trade.

THE SHIPMAN

The same inside knowledge informs the portrait of the Shipman. The first eight lines give us a picturesque sailor, suntanned, comically unfamiliar with horses. The tenth contains a wonderfully unexpected climax:

> Ful many a draughte of wyn had he ydrawe
> Fro Burdeux-ward, whil that the chapman sleep. (lines 396–7)

The sentence is innocent until the last two words deliver the sting in its tail. Chaucer, a vintner's son, repays a professional grudge. We now hear of the Shipman's method of dealing with captives, and the dagger of lines 392–3 begins to look more dangerous. The vivid glimpse of the Shipman's callousness fades, however, under the lengthy catalogue of his impressive professional skills, ending in a circumstantial point added as an afterthought, like the comment on the Cook's ability with blankmanger. Such details allow us to believe that Chaucer is recalling what the man had told him.

THE DOCTOR OF PHYSIC

The theme of food and drink, raised with the Prioress and the Monk and dominating the portrait of the Franklin, continues with the Doctor of Physic. First, however, we hear of his professional prowess – the most encyclopedic of all these lists of authorities and terms of art, a medieval convention which Chaucer seems particularly to have enjoyed. Like the Knight, he is a 'verray, parfit' example of his kind, but in his case this involves conspiracy with the apothecary against the patient – an ancient complaint against doctors. After he has displayed to us his improbably vast Arabic knowledge, we come to his diet. As we might expect from the best doctor in the world (line 412), his diet is moderate:

> But of greet norissyng and digestible.
> His studie was but litel on the Bible. (lines 437–8)

The description moves immediately to his (costly) dress, but the one-liner about the Doctor's neglect of the Bible is a shrewd thrust, as unexpected as the Shipman's nocturnal thieving. The rhyme is particularly clever, pointedly contrasting the Doctor's scrupulous and learned care for his body with his neglect of his soul. The last two couplets destroy the Doctor's character: to him the Black Death (the bubonic plague, for which there was no cure) has brought gold, gold which he is not going to pass on to others. Meanness was a vice even more unpopular in the Middle Ages than it is now. All his learning merely makes him rich. The impressive edifice is inhabited by a miser.

THE WIFE OF BATH

The liveliness of the Wife of Bath, one of Chaucer's most famous characters, comes as a relief. Her portrait is enormously amplified later on by the immensely long preamble to her tale, where she indulges in unrestrained autobiography. Her garrulous tongue is only hinted at in line 474. In her Prologue she explains her five husbands, and also two apparently inconsequential points of the portrait – her deafness (line 446) and the connection between her wandering and her teeth (lines 467–8). The illogicality of the narrator's *but* in line 446 is characteristic of him – she was a good woman but unfortunately rather deaf. The deafness is, however, a significant detail, the result of a blow on the ear from her fifth husband. He had been reading to her from an encyclopedic work on the faults of women, when she knocked him into the fire and tore three leaves from his book; he struck her on the ear, but was so alarmed when she fainted that she was able to make him promise to give her sovereignty in the marriage. In medieval theory and law, biblical in origin, the man is the head of the woman, and should be obeyed. The Wife, however, is not receptive to this doctrine, and her deafness is **symbolic** of this unwillingness to listen. Physical characteristics in these portraits often have a moral import. Thus the Wife explains in her Prologue:

> Gat-tothed I was, and that bicam me weel:
> I hadde the prente of seinte Venus seel.

(I was gate-toothed, which became me well: I had the print of St Venus's seal.)

Medieval students of physiology held that to have teeth widely spaced (gate-toothed) was a sign of boldness, falseness, gluttony and lasciviousness; the Wife, born under Venus (who was no saint), regards it as confirming her venereal nature. The Wife's 'gate' teeth gave her many opportunities to wander off the road. It is characteristic of Chaucer that these two apparently irrelevant physical details are made to seem even more casual by being qualified by, 'and that was scathe' and 'soothly for to seye' – the fill-in or tag phrases of his chatty narrative.

The Wife's portrait begins with a standard feature of the dreadful women whom clerks (and comic writers) in the Middle Ages liked to caricature. She is self-important and vain (lines 449–52) in exactly the same way as the wives of the Guildsmen (lines 376–8). This liking for display is cleverly combined by Chaucer with her profession (cloth-making); and her vanity in church (a scandal to clerics) is treated with the hyperbole of *roialliche* (line 378), but here carried to magnificent heights of absurdity. The Church required that at Mass women should cover their heads, lest their hair distract the men. The Wife's coverchiefs, of her own manufacture, weigh ten pound (or so it is reported). Her stockings are scarlet and tight-laced, and her shoes are 'moyste and newe'. She is thus the scarlet woman, flaunting her wares, whom the preachers against female vanity loved to hate. But – and this is very Chaucerian – she is both sexually attractive and at the same time ridiculously overdressed. Her face is bold and red (the colour of Mars) but also *fair* (comely).

The Wife turns out to be the monster of anti-feminist comedy – aggressive, nagging, gossiping, lustful, vain, wasteful, domineering. Yet she is not unattractive. She is also more human than any stereotype, and many find her lovable in her overflowing vanity. In the General Prologue, she is primarily a comic figure. The touches of hyperbole at the beginning of her portrait are followed by a series of hints that her amorous adventures have been epically excessive. Apart from her five husbands and other youthful company we are told that she had 'passed many a straunge strem' and knew a lot about 'wandrynge by the weye'. These nudges and winks from Chaucer are continued in the details of her easy riding, her spurs, and finally:

Of remedies of love she knew per chaunce

For she koude of that art the olde daunce. (lines 475–6)

The *remedies* and *olde daunce* do not suggest virtue. All in all, she is quite a contrast to the chastity, modesty and refinement of the Prioress.

Finally, the Wife's portrait contains symbolic details of a sort that appears increasingly in the satirical portraits of the lower characters. Thus, the redness of her face, her hat as broad as a shield and her sharp spurs all suggest her martial qualities. In the miniature portrait of her in the Ellesmere Manuscript she carries a whip to beat her husbands.

GOOD MEN

THE PARSON AND THE PLOUGHMAN

The Parson is 'a good man' but good in a different way from the 'good Wife'. The Wife is *worthy:* she has had five husbands. The Merchant is' *worthy;* and the Manciple is *gentil.* Yet these adjectives have also been applied to the Knight. We are invited to discriminate between moral worth and social worth. Chaucer points out that the poor Parson is spiritually rich, and does not call him 'a good felawe'.

The goodness of the Parson and the Ploughman sets them apart from the social world through which we have been descending. They are described in terms of their virtues rather than their physical appearance, diet or tastes. Idealists are thus described idealistically, just as materialists have been described in material terms. The contrast is absolute. Both brothers' characters are formed directly upon the ideals of the Church and the Gospel. Unlike the professionals and their servants, and unlike many clerics, they give rather than take, they love God and their neighbour, work hard for others, and are humble. Although such men were as rare as saints, their ideals are clearly believed in. There is energy as well as piety in both descriptions, and they are made persuasive by the same colloquial actuality that animates the other portraits. The Parson was 'loth to curse', he caught the words out of the gospel, he ran not to London, his speech was not 'daungerous ne digne'. The Ploughman was 'a trewe swynkere' and loved God 'thogh him gamed or smerte'. The Parson is developed beyond an ideal, and if Knight, Parson and Ploughman represent medieval social ideals, the Parson is the most fully realised. A 'noble example', he is also a real village priest: if the Ploughman carts dung, it is the Parson who speaks of *a shiten shepherd*. Chaucer further applies the **metaphor** of *clennesse* to gold and to the mire which encumbers the sheep. Christ's pastoral parables are made at home in the land of England. This shepherd is benign (lines 483, 518):

> To drawen folk to hevene by fairnesse,
> By good ensample, this was his bisynesse. (lines 519–20)

He is not overscrupulous, but is prepared to snub obstinacy when necessary – as he does the Host at the end of the pilgrimage.

STEWARDS

The last six pilgrims are introduced as a group. What have they in common? All except Chaucer are dishonest stewards who defraud those they serve, and abuse positions of trust. They are criticised with a less friendly irony.

THE MILLER

There was broad comedy in the portrait of the Wife of Bath, not without mild vulgarity. The Miller, however, is a grotesque figure, coarse and menacing. His description is unprecedentedly physical, partly because his brutal strength is the key to his character (he is a bully) and partly because of the satirical tradition of caricaturing vice as gross and beastly. A powerful physical presence is immediately suggested, and there follow sundry unattractive details of his features, with a final mixture of remarks on his habits and dress. Closer attention to the portrait, however, transforms this 'realistic' physical portrait into a moral emblem.

Discord is suggested by wrestling, door-smashing, weapons and *jangling* (line 560). A procession led by bagpipes may not prove harmonious. Even the Miller's profession involves breaking and crushing. Bestial affinities are suggested by the brawn, bones, ram, sow, fox, and sow's ears (out of which, according to the old English proverb, silk purses cannot be made). The hairs on the wart on the top of his nose are red, as are his beard and his huge mouth, whereas his nostrils are black. These last details seem sinister, even hellish: the Devil's mouth is portrayed in medieval painting as the gaping mouth of a furnace. The

Miller's brutality makes more impression than his dishonesty or his dirty mind.

THE MANCIPLE
The Manciple, by contrast, is *gentil,* but a thief of others' food, like the Miller, if more discreetly. Discretion and prudence are ironically described as *wise* in line 569 and *wisdom* in line 575. In this wise buying, the Manciple emulates the wise purchasing of the Sergeant of the Law (line 318). The narrator is amused by seeing the legal defrauders legally defrauded by their uneducated servant, as becomes clear with the last line. The Manciple is not individualised – he is a faceless man.

THE REEVE
The Reeve is mean in every sense. He is scrawny, unlike the Miller, and angry, unlike the Manciple. In other respects he resembles the Manciple, whose lines 579–86 also apply to the Reeve: he cheats his lord in a way that the lord cannot detect. He is also like the Miller in that he oppresses those below him (lines 603–5). Millers were the natural enemies of reeves and of carpenters, and the Reeve is a carpenter too. They ride at opposite ends of the pilgrimage.

  The three dishonest stewards are thus closely linked by similarities and contrasts. The antipathy of the Miller and the Reeve prepares us for their tales, which immediately follow the Knight's and set in motion the dramatic conflicts which animate the *Tales* thereafter. Yet the Reeve's portrait has touches rich beyond the necessities of any future dramas. There are few more varied passages in the Prologue than lines 603–12. The Reeve's professional skills become sinister in line 605, and the deathly fear in which he is held casts an ironic light upon the setting of his house: 'With grene trees yshadwed was his place', although green was not always a good colour in medieval lore. His lord's kindness to him and his own cruelty to his inferiors may echo New Testament parables. But the Reeve's cunning manipulation of his lord is a Chaucerian theme: the Reeve takes pleasure in being thanked by his victim (line 612). This expresses the age's disgust at hypocrisy, and a Gothic taste for dramatic reversal. One of Chaucer's most famous lines is 'The smylere with the knyf under the cloke' (Knight's Tale, line 1998).

ECCLESIASTICAL VILLAINS

Last come the precious pair of Ecclesiastical villains whom even the charitable Chaucer, who can hate the sin but love the sinner, derides.

THE SUMMONER

The Summoner is the simpler of the two: a lecher, a drunkard, a corrupt officer of the law, easily bribed by a drink from a fellow-criminal; demanding bribes from those who prefer their purses to their souls; corrupting the young. The opinion that a writ of imprisonment is worse than an excommunication (because it costs money) is the Summoner's. Chaucer does not as a rule openly attribute opinions to his characters but rather seems to report them. The Summoner, like the Pardoner, does not believe in what he does. Sarcasm rather than irony is the note, as in the comments on the Summoner's Latin (lines 637–46) and his kindness (lines 647–65). Lechery is his ruling passion: his face is *fyr-reed* (line 624) and he is *hoot* (line 626). This is shown by his facial acne and his love of hot foods and strong drink. For him, *wyn* rhymes with *Latyn* (line 638) and *concubyn* (line 650). Bread and wine appear in the last couplet, and it may be that, as in the Pardoner's Tale, these are connected with the inability of the sinner to partake of communion. Excommunication was the ultimate penalty of the court the Summoner served.

THE PARDONER

The Pardoner is sillier and more corrupt than the cunning but stupid Summoner. He sings alto to the Summoner's bass, and he is physically a eunuch, an incomplete man (line 691). This explains not just his affected hairstyle, but his carrying the (false) pardons or bulls in his lap as a compensating source of potency. His lack of masculinity symbolises the inefficacy of what he sells.

The Pardoner has false relics, which fool the ignorant country folk into giving him money which should go to the parish priest. He preaches well, as he later explains, because his takings depend upon it. The Pardoner's own Prologue and Tale dramatically illustrate in detail how he uses his relics, how he preaches and tells a story, and how he blackmails the guilty and ignorant into buying his pardons. The Host, however, exposes the sterile nature of the Pardoner's false bulls from Rome, and exposes him also as a eunuch. The Pardoner is contemptible because he defrauds the poor, like a crooked insurance salesman, but he is doubly unwelcome on the pilgrimage, because he usurps the function of the Parson. Pardoners could not pardon sins, nor were they licensed to preach. This Pardoner was probably not a cleric, did not come from Rome, sold false pardons and, as his Tale shows, did not believe in the pardons he professed to sell. He was thus a complete fraud. By a significant irony, the theme of his sermon is *'Radix malorum est cupiditas'* ('the love of money is the root of all evils'). He is not a pilgrim but a dangerous parasite, a wolf in sheep's clothing. Hence he is symbolically made a eunuch of repugnant appearance – a fit partner for the corrupt ecclesiastical policeman who aids and abets him. The Pardoner, like the Wife of Bath, is a character developed much more fully in his Prologue.

From this review of the portraits emerge the themes of avarice and human self-ignorance. Gratitude and penitence, which in the end the Parson starkly recalls to the minds of the pilgrims, do not seem to be uppermost in the minds of most of the pilgrims or the Host. But only the Pardoner is there simply to make money out of the others. The loathing felt for the Pardoner's absolute falsity, and the fervour of the Parson's portrait, imply faith. Chaucer detests the mercenary and loves the true shepherd (line 514). Toward those clerics who fall between the two – the Nun, Monk and Friar – he is subtly, broadly or keenly satirical. In many of the other portraits his comic vision is mediated by means of an irony that allows much flexibility in interpretation.

What conclusions about Chaucer's view of medieval society can be drawn from the Prologue portraits? It was not, of course, Chaucer's purpose to present an analysis of society for the modern historian, but to introduce a work of fiction. The portraits of the pilgrims are presented through the medium of a very impressionable social persona whose values do not always represent the author's deeper views. Thus, Chaucer agrees that the Monk is right to do no work (lines 186–8), but he also makes us doubt the truth of this. His own views are hard to ascertain, except at the extremes. It is clear that we are to admire the Knight, Parson and Ploughman, but not the Summoner or the Pardoner. Attitudes to the pilgrims in between vary from indulgence (the Squire), to irony (the Doctor) and satire. Such views are not new, but their indirect and humorous method of delivery is, and the effect is both more engaging and thought-provoking than direct satire.

THE ROAD TO CANTERBURY

The remainder of the Prologue looks forward to the tale-telling competition and the pilgrimage. After the detail of the portraits, Chaucer reestablishes his **persona** as an amiable bumbler, confiding to the audience: 'My wit is short, ye may well understonde.' Humility is the poet's favourite guise.

THE HOST

The Host recreates the merry cheer which was a medieval social ideal. Having feasted the pilgrims (and received payment), he proposes a game which will increase their mirth – and cost them nothing (line 668). In fact it is to cost all but one of them the price of another supper at the Tabard on their return. The Host, as president of the game, will be able to play the part of 'a marchal in an halle' for which his physique and talents fit him well. He thus secures custom, profit for himself, diversion and what today might be called an ego-trip. While we note the Host's shrewdness and dexterity in stage-managing this takeover, we are also impressed by his good humour. He captures the good will of the pilgrims by flattery and exuberance and with a masterly sales talk. Had the pilgrimage gone according to the Host's plan, he would have had 'a thank and yet a cote and hood', like the Reeve. Unlike the Reeve, however, he seems a good fellow.

One consequence of the Host's cheery ultimatum is that the pilgrimage is transformed, without our noticing it, into a party game. The pilgrim narrator enjoys good company, and may have no objection, but not all the pilgrims may have been equally happy with the promise into which they had been so innocently hustled – the Prioress, the Parson, the Miller and the Pardoner might all have different objections. But the Host manages it so that we hear nothing of objections, but only of ease, mirth, merriment, disport, comfort, wine and ale. Also that anyone who disobeys him will have to pay the expenses of the others, and that the prize supper will be at a fixed price. It is notable, however, that in the arrangements for the competition (lines 790–801), the tales are to be 'of aventures that whilom han bifalle' – the Host's idea of a story – but that the prize will go to him who tells 'tales of best sentence and moost solaas', which is quite another idea, perhaps more like the poet's own.

The Host remains an unknown quantity. His original description tells us less than his behaviour, but even this remains finally elusive. *The Canterbury Tales* has already begun to develop on dramatic lines quite different from the static descriptions we have passed through. Our guides, Chaucer as narrator and the Host as master of the game, are both unpredictable.

The setting-out at dawn has narrative verve. The manly Host leads forth his flock at a quiet pace, sternly reminds them of their oaths of obedience, and, while the horses are watered, bids the pilgrims draw. He politely invites the senior gentleman and lady present to draw, but jokingly presses the retiring Clerk to submit himself also to the dominion of chance; and rounds up the others.

It seems that the Host may have fixed the cut so that the Knight gets the short straw. The narrator is delighted by this fortunate turn of events. The Host has thus at the outset involved the most honoured and authoritative of the pilgrims. The Knight proves to be a good sport, and jovially agrees to tell the first tale. The pilgrimage is forgotten and the game has begun.

CHRISTIAN COMEDY

Chaucer is a comic writer with a rich sense of humanity, yet *The Canterbury Tales* is more than a human comedy: it is, as Dryden said, God's plenty. Comedy in the medieval sense of the word means a story with a happy ending. At the end of his great *Troilus and Criseyde* (which he calls 'litel myn tragedye'), Chaucer prays that God will send him the ability to try his hand in 'some comedye'. Dante (1265–1321) had entitled his pilgrimage through Hell and Purgatory to Heaven the *Commedia*, not because it was humorous but because it ends in a happier state than it began. Chaucer's *Tales* are a large and varied work, where the part obscures the whole, where we shift between tellers and their tales, and where the design is not completed. However, the pilgrimage is more than a device. The Parson, 'a good man of religioun', tells the last tale, late in the evening as the shadows are lengthening. It is an uncompromising treatise on the necessity for repentance, and comes as a shock. In retrospect, after the Knight's 'noble storie', the pleasant pilgrimage can be seen to have declined into a comic, quarrelsome, blasphemous and sometimes brutal chaos, the lowest point of which is the Cook's drunken fall from his horse into the slough. As the pilgrims near Canterbury, their fallibility appears. The Parson asks Jesus for his grace: 'To shewe yow the wey, in this viage, / Of thilke parfit glorious pilgrymage, / That highte Jerusalem celestial'.

Here the Parson is speaking **allegorically**: the way to the heavenly Jerusalem is by the path of repentance – a straight and narrow way unlike the broad and easy road to Canterbury. There are many glimpses, hints and reminders of this 'high way' among the more sinful as well as the more pious tales. Nevertheless, despite the comic delight in and understanding of human self-delusion, and despite all its abounding charity towards the sinner, Chaucer's human world is organised by the Christian hatred of sin made explicit only in the Parson's Tale.

The General Prologue is so sunny, sane, earthly and human that it may be necessary to emphasise that although Chaucer has been called the first humanist in English literature and the first realist in portraying personal and social relations, he remains also a medieval Christian in his sense of the impermanence of this human life which seems so real. This appears only obliquely in the Prologue, which is largely static, with little dramatic interaction between the characters, but the claims of Christ colour the opening and the portraits of the Knight, Parson and Ploughman.

The perennial Christian philosophy is economically expressed outside the *Tales* in the poem of Chaucer's which appears most often in manuscripts, *Truth*, or the *Balade de Bon Conseyl*. Italicised final -*e* is to be sounded.

> Flee fro the prees, and dwelle with sothfastness*e*,
> Suffyce unto thy good, though it be smal;
> For hord hath hate, and climbing tikelness*e*,
> Prees hath envye, and wele blent overal;
> Savour no more than thee bihov*e* shal;

Reule wel thyself, that other folk canst rede;
And trouthe thee shal delivere, it is no drede.

Tempest thee noght al croked to redresse,
In trust of hir that turneth as a bal:
Gret reste stant in litel besinesse;
Be war also to sporne ayeyns an al;
Stryve not, as doth the crokke with the wal.
Daunte thyself, that dauntest otheres dede;
And trouthe thee shal delivere, it is no drede.

That thee is sent, receyve in buxumnesse;
The wrastling for this world axeth a fal.
Her is non hoom, her nis but wildernesse:
Forth, pilgrim, forth! Forth, beste, out of thy stal!
Know thy contree, look up, thank God of al;
Hold the heye wey, and lat thy gost thee lede;
And trouthe thee shal delivere, it is no drede.

This can be literally rendered:

Leave the throng of Court and make your home with Truth; content yourself with
what you have, though it be slender. For hoarding is attended by hatred and
worldly preferment by precariousness; the Court is full of envy, and success quite
blinds its possessor. Relish no more than what shall become you; govern yourself
well, that you may counsel others; and Truth shall most certainly deliver you.
Do not torment yourself to reform all that is amiss, putting your trust in her who
turns like a ball. Great peace is to be found in little business; beware also of kicking
against the pricks; do not strive as does the pot against the wall. Tame yourself,
you who tame the actions of others, and Truth shall most certainly deliver you.
Accept with a good will what is sent you: wrestling for this world asks for a fall.
There is no home here; here is nothing but a wilderness: out, pilgrim, out! Out,
beast, out of thy stall! Acknowledge your native land – look up, thank God for
everything. Stick to the high road and let your spirit lead you; and Truth shall
assuredly deliver you.

This advice comes from a man who seems quite at home in this world. It
may be that Chaucer himself had discovered that 'The wrastling for this
world axeth a fal'. But the philosophy is traditional – it has been described
as a resumé of the *Consolation of Philosophy* of Boethius (AD *c.*480–524),

one of the most popular and influential books of the Middle Ages, and a work which Chaucer translated. The *Consolation* is itself a resumé of Stoic and Platonic thinking on the Contempt of the World, as it was called in Christian tradition. Stoicism was a widespread classical philosophical and ethical system of thought centred on obedience to natural law. Plato (*c.*429–347BC) taught that the world of physical appearances and events is unreal. Chaucer's Bon Conseyl, or Good Advice, is to scorn the rewards of this world in order to earn those of the next, which is the homeland of the soul: 'Know thy contree'. The truth which shall set free the friend to whom the poem is written is the truth of St John's Gospel 8:32: 'Ye shall know the truth, and the truth shall make you free'. The philosophy of *Truth* is a synthesis of classical and Christian moral thought, in which biblical allusions mingle with classical maxims in a proverbial style which may surprise us if we think of the Middle Ages as unfamiliar with classical tradition. The Sermon on the Mount of line 2 and the conversion of Saul (line 11) combine quite happily with Fortune (line 9), a classical goddess unknown to the Bible. The God who is to be thanked (line 19) is the God of Christian revelation, but the sentiments of the first two stanzas of the poem would be familiar to an educated Roman pagan. The fundamental image of the poem is of life as a pilgrimage – a medieval image but not necessarily an ascetic one, as can be seen in the homely and humorous image of the pilgrim as a beast (line 18) to be led by its soul, as a cow is by the cowherd.

Truth can serve as a mini-introduction to the General Prologue, not only because it is a summary of the moral commonplaces of the age, but because it presents the human being as a pilgrim (from Latin *peregrinus*, wanderer). The famous first paragraph of the Prologue is full of classical mythology and the Arabic astronomy of the Zodiac, and also of the natural history of a scientific sort, which places Nature (line 11) in an apparently sovereign position. Yet the sentence ends with the simple piety of the English pilgrimage to Canterbury. It would be equally mistaken to ignore either the naturalism of the introduction or the supernaturalism of the conclusion. The two are blended in the rich synthesis of *Truth*, and in the same blend of an elevated and a homely style. Medieval Christianity was not the religion only of monks and ascetics: the whole of what we now think of as secular society was included in the Incarnation, as was the natural world of bird and 'holt and heeth'. The spring which keeps the birds awake all night also moves folks to go on pilgrimage to thank the saint who has interceded for them when they were sick. The poet is at home in the physical world which he celebrates, but which, as he reminds us, we must ultimately leave behind.

VARIETY AND UNITY

The Canterbury Tales combines in a simple narrative many varied and dramatic subjects of human interest, from the loftiest to the lowest. Factors unifying its very diverse materials include:

(1) The narrative **frame-stories** of the pilgrimage and tale-telling;
(2) The role of the Host as master of ceremonies;
(3) The personality and voice of the narrator, Chaucer the poet and pilgrim;
(4) The dramatic interplay between the characters of the pilgrims, either because their values differ – the Miller's bawdy mocks the Knight's idealism – or because they are professional rivals – the Friar and the Summoner, rival parasites upon the laity, tell tales against each other;
(5) Intellectual debate, for example on the subject of authority in marriage, the theme of the Wife's Tale and the Clerk's Tale;
(6) An underlying Christian humanism.

The fourth and fifth of these factors do not come out in the Prologue, which introduces the first and second. The third and sixth may be examined in a discussion of the strategy of the Prologue's three parts: the pilgrimage, the pilgrims, and the tale-telling game. The middle part, the pilgrim portraits, is the most substantial thing in the Prologue, but the way we approach it is considerably affected by the narrative sections which frame it.

STYLE

If *The Canterbury Tales* were written today the Prologue would probably be in prose, although some of the Tales require the artifice of verse.

Chaucer's own prose was rudimentary compared with his verse, as can be seen in his prose Tale of Melibee and the Parson's Tale. The Prologue is written in rhyming **pentameters** and in a direct, colloquial, flexible style. It is spoken aloud by the poet to his audience and purports to record his actual experience. Its verse does not go in for the elevation and use of imagery and allusion which are sometimes thought characteristic of poetry, although the opening is formal and later there is the occasional telling use of **simile**.

The language is clear, rapid, almost transparent. It draws no attention to itself except when the narrator apologises for his inadequacies or uses unusually excessive padding (such as 'for the nonys' and 'soothly for to seye'). Chaucer's expository style in the Prologue is a model of simplicity and unaffected unselfconscious elegance: it gives the illusion of a varied stream of discourse, lively, free from artifice or vulgarity. Although so old, it seems fresh, even naïve at times; this quaintness is the result of unfamiliarity, for although Chaucer is engaging and can be captivating, he was a civilised, courtly and urbane writer. If his age was simpler in its spirit and technology, it was sophisticated as well as earthy. A naïve customs officer is a contradiction in terms: the naïve narrator is a deliberate pose of Chaucer's.

Some of Chaucer's best lines are off-hand yet deadly. If art is to conceal art, Chaucer's art is to seem artless. Many of the casual reflections of his narrator are tellingly accurate:

> And yet he seemed bisier than he was (line 322)

> or

> But sooth to seyn, I noot how men him calle (line 284)

> or

> They were adrad of hym as of the deeth (line 605)

This style can do whatever is required of it. This reflects a familiarity with his public that no subsequent author has exceeded: Chaucer like Shakespeare was both sophisticated and popular, but his language is less extravagant, partly because members of medieval society had a lot in common with each other.

The Prologue is verse rather than poetry. Its most easily pinpointed quality is its crisp rhyming, as in the self-contained couplet:

He was not pale as a forpyned goost:

A fat swan loved he best of any roost. (lines 205–6)

where the association of the rhyme-words is quite unexpected, and a comic contrast is made. Or the couplet can be open, and run on:

She was so charitable and so pitous

She wolde wepe, if that she saugh a mous

Kaught in a trappe ... (lines 143–4)

Where *mous* defines the Nun's pity as directed towards small animals, rather than towards people as 'charity' had suggested. Many of the best rhymes are for the purposes of bathos or ironic wit, reversing the expectations of the previous line. Particularly audacious are *digestible/Bible* (lines 437–8), *Bathe/scathe* (lines 445–6), *cloystre/oystre* (lines 181–2), *hoot/goot* (lines 687–8) and *bledde/fedde/deed/breed* (lines 145–9). Each rhyme is a witty comment. The element of hyperbole, or deliberate exaggeration, seen in many of the images of food, dress or physique, also appears in the spectacular skill with which Chaucer sometimes divides a couplet between two utterly disconnected subjects (and so connects them). This is seen at the end of one portrait and the beginning of the next, as at lines 207–8, 269–70 and 387–8; or in the concluding rhyme of many portraits. It is at the rhymes that we feel the sharpness beneath Chaucer's easy tone.

Whether writing about the Prologue's style or themes, its structure or its social satire, it is best to quote a significant detail, a telling line or even a single word, such as *frosty* (line 268) or *roialliche* (line 378). All generalisations about the Prologue, and especially about Chaucer's attitude to society, sound heavy and dull compared with the lightness of his own words.

PART FOUR

Textual analysis

TEXT 1   THE OPENING SENTENCE

(A rough rule for the pronunciation of final -*e* is to pronounce it only when it is required by the rhyme or metre. It is not pronounced when the next word begins with a vowel. Pronounce '*e*' when *italicised.*)

> Whan that Aprill with his shoures soot*e*
> The droghte of March hath perc*ed* to the root*e*,
> And bathed every veyne in swich licour
> Of which vertu engendred is the flour;
> 5 Whan Zephirus eek with his sweet*e* breeth
> Inspir*ed* hath in every holt and heeth
> The tendr*e* cropp*es*, and the yong*e* sonn*e*
> Hath in the Ram his half cours yronn*e*,
> And smal*e* fowel*es* maken melody*e*,
> 10 That slepen al the nyght with open y*e*
> (So priketh hem nature in hir corages),
> Thanne longen folk*e* to goon on pilgrimages,
> And palmeres for to seken straung*e* strond*es*,
> To fern*e* halw*es*, kowthe in sondry lond*es*;
> 15 And specially from every shir*es* end*e*
> Of Eng*e*lond to Caunterbury they wend*e*,
> The hooly blisful martir for to sek*e*,
> That hem hath holpen whan that they were seek*e*. (lines 1–18)

The Prologue has a fresh and joyful beginning: the spring urges the natural world into growth, birds into song and human beings to go on pilgrimage. These signs of spring are conveyed in a sentence of four clauses. The clauses are concerned with time (*Whan* in lines 1 and 5, *Thanne* in line 12), and then with place: *And specially* in line 15. The clauses address in turn the meteorological, vegetable, animal and human. This rhetorical device is called a **chronographia**, a literary setting in time and place; Chaucer had read such elevated openings to many of the Cantos of Dante's *Divine Comedy*, and he is imitating them. This sentence is far more formal than the rest of the Prologue, not only in its length and complex structure and phrasing (*in swich licour / Of which vertu engendred is* ...), but also in its initial vocabulary which is scientific, mythological and astronomical. The references are explained in the Detailed Commentaries. The sentence opens slowly and grandly, becomes lively with the *tendre croppes, the yonge sonne* and the *smale foweles* that cannot sleep, and finally comes home to human beings, and to Chaucer's home county of Kent. It is Nature that makes people *long* to go on pilgrimages, a natural instinct directed to a supernatural end: gratitude for the saint's intercession in heaven for those who have been sick but are now whole and healthy.

TEXT 2　　THE PRIORESS

Ther was also a Nonne, a PRIORESS*E*,
That of hir smylyng was ful symple and coy;
120　Hire gretteste ooth was but by Seint*e* Loy;
And she was cleped madame Eglentyn*e*.
Ful weel she soong the servic*e* dyvyn*e*,
Entun*ed* in hir nose ful sem*e*ly;
And Frenssh she spak ful faire and fetisly,
125　After the scole of Stratford att*e* Bow*e*,
For Frenssh of Parys was to hire unknow*e*.
At met*e* wel ytaught was she with all*e*;
She leet no morsel from hir lipp*es* fall*e*,
Ne wette hir fyngres in hir sauc*e* dep*e*;
130　Wel koude she carie a morsel and wel kep*e*
That no drop*e* ne fill*e* upon hire brest.
In curteisi*e* was set ful muchel hir lest.
Hir over-lipp*e* wyp*ed* she so clen*e*
That in hir copp*e* ther was no ferthyng sen*e*
135　Of grec*e*, whan she dronken hadde hir draught*e*.
Ful sem*e*ly after hir met*e* she raught*e*.
And sikerly she was of greet desport,
And ful plesaunt, and amyable of port,
And peyned hire to countrefet*e* cheer*e*

140 Of court, and to been estatlich of maner*e*,
    And to ben holden digne of reverenc*e*.
    But for to speken of hire conscienc*e*,
    She was so charitable and so pitous
    She wolde wepe, if that she saugh a mous
145 Kaught in a trappe, if it were deed or bledd*e*.
    Of smal*e* houndes hadde she that she fedd*e*
    With rosted flessh, or milk and wastel-breed.
    But soor*e* wept*e* she if oon of hem were deed,
    Or if men smoot it with a yerd*e* smert*e*;
150 And al was conscience and tendre hert*e*.
    Ful semyly hir wympul pynch*ed* was,
    Hir nose tretys, hir eyen greye as glas,
    Hir mouth ful smal, and therto softe and reed.
    But sikerly she hadde a fair forheed;
155 It was almoost a spann*e* brood, I trow*e*;
    For, hardily, she was nat undergrow*e*.
    Ful fetys was hir cloke, as I was war.
    Of smal coral aboute hire arm she bar
    A peire of bed*es*, gauded al with gren*e*,
160 And theron heng a brooch of gold ful sheen*e*,
    On which ther was first write a crown*ed* A,
    And after *Amor vincit omnia.* (lines 118–62)

This portrait is selected as a sample of Chaucer's art and of the problems of interpretation and tone set by his habit of praise. It is hard to assess the degree of criticism in the portrait, an assessment complicated by changes in the meaning of words and by modern unfamiliarity with the ideals and historical realities of the life of nuns. Such factors – ironical praise, changes in sense, and historical ignorance – play a part in interpreting almost all the portraits.

Deficiency of knowledge may be remedied more easily than prejudice. Religious orders were suppressed at the Protestant Reformation of the sixteenth century, and many people of today, even among Christians, may have little understanding or experience of the ideal of the celibate single life dedicated to Christ. Since Prioresses often came from aristocratic families or gentry, ladylike bearing and courtly table manners are no surprise. Most *gentil* families had members in religious orders; Chaucer has a sister or a daughter who was a nun.) Madame Eglentyne's name, nose, eyes, mouth and forehead are well bred. Little dogs and gold brooches were not in the Benedictine Rule; yet the Rule had been modified over the centuries; the Prioress's little weaknesses do not in themselves indicate personal laxity. Key words which have changed sense are *coy*, which means 'quiet' not 'archly inviting'; *countrefete* means 'imitate' not 'fake'. These considerations make the portrait less broadly satiric and more ironic.

But ambiguity is systematic. We have to recognise the ambiguities rather than hope to resolve them all. The motto on the brooch could be either religious or secular (see Detailed Commentaries). We are to smile at the nun's French accent, too-perfect manner and pity for very small animals, but whether her nasal singing, her height and her large forehead deserve a smile is not so clear (large foreheads, for example, were fashionably beautiful in the late fourteenth century). The question is complicated by the recurrent use in the portraits of hyperbole and the superlative. Chaucer's work often shows amusement at human vanity generally, not just feminine vanity. But how gentle is this satire, and how severe? Madame Eglentyne is certainly too concerned with manner, and seems to care more for mice than for men. The society lady's devotion to pets is an enduring comic stereotype. Older critical reaction is summed up in a phrase of the critic John Livingstone Lowes: 'the engagingly imperfect submergence of the feminine in the ecclesiastical'. Recent views of this portrait have been affected by outrage at the antisemitism of the Tale the Prioress later tells. But to see this nun and everything about her as ridiculous or worse would be a serious mistake. Chaucer is judgemental only in extreme cases. He does not here repudiate the celibate ideal, nor does he condemn the nun's softness. He carefully leaves plenty of room for interpretation. We too have to listen carefully – and we do not have to make up our minds.

TEXT 3   THE FRANKLIN

A FRANKELEYN was in his compaigny*e*.
Whit was his berd as is the dayesy*e*;

Of his complexioun he was sangwyn.
Wel loved he by the morwe a sop in wyn;
335 To lyven in delit was evere his wone,
For he was Epicurus owene sone,
That heeld opinioun that pleyn delit
Was verray felicitee parfit.
An housholdere, and that a greet, was he;
340 Seint Julian he was in his contree.
His breed, his ale, was alweys after oon;
A bettre envyned man was nowher noon.
Withoute bake mete was nevere his hous,
Of fissh and flessh, and that so plentevous
345 It snewed in his hous of mete and drynke;
Of alle deyntees that men koude thynke,
After the sondry sesons of the yeer,
So chaunged he his mete and his soper.
Ful many a fat partrich hadde he in muwe,
350 And many a breem and many a luce in stuwe.
Wo was his cook but if his sauce were
Poynaunt and sharp, and redy al his geere.
His table dormant in his halle alway
Stood redy covered al the longe day.
355 At sessiouns ther was he lord and sire;
Ful ofte tyme he was knyght of the shire.
An anlaas and a gipser al of silk
Heeng at his girdel, whit as morne milk.
A shirreve hadde he been, and a contour.
360 Was nowher swich a worthy vavasour. (lines 331–60)

It is a good exercise to try to make a literal translation of selected passages of this short text. Here is an attempt to do so for this portrait:

> In his company was a Franklin. His beard was as white as a daisy; he was sanguine of complexion. In the morning he dearly loved a cake dipped in wine. Always to live in pleasure was his settled habit, for he was a true son of Epicurus, who held the view that true and perfect happiness consisted in pleasure itself. He was a householder, and a great one: in his part of the world he was St Julian. His bread

and his ale were always of the same quality; and nowhere was there a man with a better cellar. His house was never without baked dishes of fish and flesh, and they were in such plenty that in his house it snowed meat and drink, and all conceivable delicacies. He changed his diet and his table according to the various seasons of the year. He had a great many fat partridges in coops, and many a bream and many a pike in ponds. It was a bad day for his cook if his sauce was not piquant and sharp, or if his equipment was not ready. There was always a table, covered and set, standing in his hall all day long. At the Quarter Sessions he was lord and master and sat many times as Knight of the Shire. A dagger, and a purse made all of white silk as white as morning milk hung from his belt. He had been a sheriff and an auditor. Nowhere was there such a splendid landholder.

This landholder does not live off the community, as many of the professionals do. He is as hospitable as St Julian, the patron saint of hospitality: his table stands there for all who come. But he is also an epicure: his delicious food is for himself (although it is the philosopher Epicurus, not the Franklin, who is said to be dedicated to pleasure – *delit.*) The old man shows the same gusto in life that makes even the most wayward pilgrim so enjoyable. The Franklin's way of life is picturesquely described, with poetic figures (lines 332, 345–6, 358); the final lines list the public offices that had brought the Sergeant into contact with him.

The picture of country hospitality, the first of many in English, is done with a Chaucerian combination of cordiality, freshness, slight hyperbole ('It *snewed* in his hous of mete and drynke') and affectionate mockery, as in:

> Ful many a fat partrich hadde he in muwe,
> And many a breem and many a luce in stuwe. (lines 349–50)

It is at the rhyme that the wit becomes apparent:

> Whit was his berd as is a dayseye.
> Of his complexioun he was sangwyn.
> Wel loved he by the morwe a sop in wyn. (lines 332–4)

The simple, factual lines succeed each other without criticism, yet the rhyming of *sangwyn* with *wyn* suggests that the wine may have helped the blood in producing the Franklin's ruddy complexion. (Such identical rhyme was admired.) The good living of the Franklin, even his testiness towards his cook, is regarded indulgently, if one can go by the innocence of the comparisons to the daisy and morning milk. The Franklin is both attractive and a caricature; such an engaging combination shows Chaucer's grasp and his humanity.

Opposite
Portrait miniature in the Ellesmere Manuscript of *The Canterbury Tales* (*c.* 1410), showing Chaucer riding along the road to Canterbury. A *penner* or pencase hangs around his neck, signifying that he is a writer. He points to the beginning of his second tale, *The Tale of Melibee.*

PART FIVE

BACKGROUND

CHAUCER'S LIFE

Geoffrey Chaucer came from a family which rose in the world through four successive generations. The Chaucers were originally from France. Geoffrey's grandfather was a wine-merchant importing from France. Geoffrey's father, John, was also a wine-merchant in the Vintry in London. Here the poet was born in 1343–4. John once held minor court office as Butler, and Geoffrey followed him in his career as a 'king's man'. Geoffrey had a sister (or daughter) who became a nun. Both his mother and his father's mother were married three times. Long after his death, his son Thomas became one of the most important men in England.

Geoffrey was made a page to Prince Lionel, Edward III's third son. In his teens he fought in the English army in France, where he was captured; Edward III ransomed him in 1360. He is recorded as visiting Spain in 1366, a year in which he married Philippa Payne de Roet. Philippa's sister was Katherine Swynford, the mistress and later the third wife of John of Gaunt, Edward III's fourth son. In 1367 he began travelling abroad on the King's business. In 1369 he fought in Picardy for John of Gaunt. In 1372 he went to Genoa and Florence on a diplomatic mission and revisited Italy in 1378 on a mission to the Lord of Milan.

From 1374 Chaucer's career is well documented, for he became Controller of Customs and Subsidy of Wools, Skins and Hides, England's largest trade. He bought a house over Aldgate, the east gate of the City of London. In 1377 he was allowed a deputy at the Custom House and in 1385 moved to Kent, which he represented in Parliament for three years, and was also a Justice of the Peace. He was Clerk for the King's Works in 1389–90, but retired from public life after being robbed and beaten two or three times in four days.

In his last decade, Chaucer was a royal pensioner and substitute forester of the royal forest of North Petherton in Somerset, an office in which he was confirmed by Henry IV in 1399. In 1400 he took a lease on a house in the garden of Westminster Abbey, but died on 25 October and was buried in a chapel of the Abbey which has since become Poets' Corner.

LITERARY CAREER

English poetry flowered in the reign of Richard II after nearly three centuries' submergence beneath the French tradition. It was a great period of English literature in prose, in drama and especially in narrative verse. Major works include *Piers Plowman*, probably by William Langland (*c.* 1331–99?), and the anonymous *Sir Gawain and the Green Knight*, composed in **alliterative metres** deriving from Old English verse. Chaucer's metre and technique, by contrast, derive from the practice of poets in Romance languages. He wrote in English only, unlike John Gower (1330–1408), a court poet ten years his senior, who wrote in French and Latin also. There were good poets before Chaucer, and he had major contemporaries. But later poets regarded Chaucer as the first great exemplar of modern English verse. He made the French **pentameter** natural in English.

Chaucer's work falls into what have been called his French, Italian and English periods. Before 1378 he followed French traditions, translating some of the famous *Roman de la Rose*. *The Book of the Duchess* (1369), his first original work, imitates French allegorical **dream-vision** poems. Later dream-visions (*The House of Fame* and *The Parliament of Fowls*) are increasingly influenced by Italian models, and the latter, a mature piece, is a minor masterpiece. Some of *The Canterbury Tales* are 'French period', such as the Life of St Cecilia and the stories of Constance and Griselda.

Chaucer's second visit to Italy in 1378 opened his eyes to a richer tradition in the work of Dante (1275–1321), whose *Commedia* he echoes many times, and Boccaccio (1313–75) whose *Teseida* and *Filostrato* became the Knight's Tale and *Troilus and Criseyde*, among his most notable poems. In these years he also translated the *Consolation of Philosophy* of Boethius (into prose) and began *The Legend of Good Women*, his last work in the French manner; like several of his works, it remained unfinished.

Chaucer probably began *The Canterbury Tales* in 1387, after he went into Kent. The loose narrative framework enabled him to find room for some of his old stories, and to develop his dramatic and realistic abilities. This last 'English' phase contains Chaucer's most vigorous and various work. But Chaucer was a Catholic and European as well as an English poet, and early influences are present also in the later work, although this expresses more directly his own humour and the life of his time. The dream-vision tradition, for instance, informs the structure of the Prologue. *Le Roman de la Rose* informs its characterisation and its **irony**. Chaucer is the first European writer to write in English, and in the *Tales* he gives us a comprehensive view of his world and of life in all its variety.

In Chaucer's work several traditions meet – popular, learned and courtly. He was a court poet, but had readers among the learned, the clergy and the merchant class. He had scientific and philosophical interests, yet his English is rapid, clear, unaffected and natural. He often seems as close to his audience as a popular entertainer. He would have read his work to his audience, although some would have also read him in private.

CHAUCER'S WORLD

Chaucer's public experience of life was as a government servant and diplomat: not a courtier but a king's man. His friends were knights and London merchants. England passed through profound changes during his lifetime. In his childhood, England had great prestige, having beaten the Scots and the French in the victories of Crécy (1346) and Poitiers (1356). In 1360 France ceded much territory to England. In 1349 Edward III had founded the Order of the Garter, the first Order of Western chivalry.

But the Black Death of 1349 had killed a third of the people of England, and it returned in the 1360s. The resultant labour shortage disrupted the feudal economy. Edward III's costly war policy began to fail, and in old age the king became unpopular. Richard II came to the throne as a child in 1377 in a time of social unrest which in 1381 broke out in the Peasants' Revolt, in which John of Gaunt's palace was sacked and Archbishop Sudbury murdered in the street. There was also religious controversy: the Popes had been in captivity at Avignon since 1309, and in 1378 the Great Schism began, between rival claimants to the Papacy. The Oxford reformer, Wyclif, attacked Church abuses in the 1370s, and criticised Church dogma. Next to nothing of this gets into Chaucer's work. He shows us the greed of the new bourgeoisie and abuses in the Church, but his religious and social values seem those usual in his day. He was certainly discreet, as befits a diplomat and a royal servant. He flourished quietly at Richard II's court, and Henry IV, John of Gaunt's son, did not reject his father's old follower when he took the throne from Richard in 1399. The history plays of Shakespeare show Richard, murdered in 1400, as the last medieval king.

Medieval society was vertically organised like a pyramid, with King and Pope at the heads of State and Church. The social hierarchy was in theory quite clear, and its ranks had legal force. People of a lower rank could be punished for wearing the dress of a higher rank. But the old feudal system, where social standing was determined by the amount of

land a man held from the king, was giving way to a more open and
mercantile economic pattern, especially in London, where Chaucer came
from the merchant class. He was not a man of the people, but his origins
were equally remote from the nobility; there are no barons among his
pilgrims. His career gave him a wide experience of English life, and
especially the life of London, many of whose 30,000 inhabitants he must
have known. Medieval society, in spite or because of its vertical
distinctions, was communal: each of Chaucer's pilgrims, however
individual, is conceived of as typical of his craft or profession, and as
having a rank and a role in society.

The Christian Church was never far away from anything in
Chaucer's England. A theological understanding of life had since the
thirteenth century governed the interpretation put upon every physical
and moral event, however material or secular its nature – whether
meteorological, psychological or personal. Christian Europe was a
Catholic community whose language was Latin. The Church was the
same in every country, offering the same Christian social and spiritual
ideal – however incompletely realised and with whatever local differences.
Despite the strains which showed in the fourteenth century, with the
failure of the Crusades, a weakened papacy, the Black Death, and the
beginnings of less collective and more personal attitudes, there was no
alternative, secular vision of life. The culture of Christendom had long
offered an integration of social and religious ideals. It was a culture which
gave an underlying unity, simplicity and breadth to the work of this
sophisticated, adventurous and experimental writer.

RELIGIOUS LIFE

Two aspects of Catholicism may need a word of introduction:
1. Clergy are either *secular* clergy, like the Parson, who live in the world
   (either in major orders – bishop, priest, deacon – or 'clerks' in minor
   orders) or *regular* clergy. Regulars – monks, nuns and friars – bound
   themselves by a Rule and lived as a community. A regular can also be
   a priest – like Chaucer's Friar and perhaps his Monk. Friars, though
   regulars in a community, went out into the world to preach. The
   Summoner is not a cleric but a lay employee. The Pardoner may not
   have the clerical status he claims. The Knight may have been a

member of a religious military order, such as the Templars or Hospitallers, or the Teutonic Knights.

2. Penance. In the New Testament, Christ says to St Peter and the apostles: 'Whose sins you shall forgive, they are forgiven.' The Church claims that priests, as successors to the apostles, have this power to offer God's forgiveness to the sinner who truly repents and performs the penance imposed. Repentance or penitence is one aim of the pilgrimage. The Pardoner has no power to absolve the guilt of sin. He deals only in certificates of remission of penance or punishment, a crucial distinction.

MIDDLE ENGLISH

Historians divide English into Old, Middle and Modern English. Old English came to an end with the Norman Conquest of Anglo-Saxon England in 1066. The rulers of England then spoke Norman French, and scholars wrote in Latin. English was spoken by most people, and gradually became a public and literary medium in the fourteenth century. Middle English was, however, an unstable mixture of dialects, infused with thousands of words from French. It was not standardised by central usage, nor by print, and changed continuously until a more stable stage was reached about 1500, when the early Modern stage of English is taken to begin. Chaucer wrote in the London dialect, from a later version of which Modern English descends.

There is no room here for an introduction to Middle English, but here are some hints:

1. Read aloud to ascertain metre and rhyme. This also helps with meaning and with tone.
2. Pronounce all consonants fully: for example the *K* and *h* in *Knight*.
3. Consult glossaries and grammatical introductions when in doubt as to sense or grammatical function.
4. Do not assume that a word means what it means today. Appearances can deceive. The *verray parfit gentil* Knight is 'true, complete and noble', not 'very perfect and soft-hearted'; the *Person of a Toun* is a village parson, not an urban individual. Other examples are: *lustful* zestful; *coy* quiet; *lewed* ignorant: *girl* young of either sex; *catel* property; *smal* slender; *wife* woman; *wood* mad. Some words are loyal

old friends but others are *faux amis*, treacherous friends who have
changed their meanings. Words such as charity, truth, chivalry also
had complex and far-reaching senses in the Middle Ages.
5. Note common words which are used in more than one sense, such as
worthy or *gentil*, and decide on the exact sense in each instance.
6. Write your own accurate prose translation of parts of the Prologue
(see Textual Analysis, Text 3 above.)

CHAUCER'S OWN ENGLISH

The best advice that can be given to a student is to make sure that he or
she understands as accurately as possible exactly what Chaucer's words
mean. Without an informed response to sense, there can be no sensitivity
to qualities of language, nor to the poet's tone of voice. Chaucer's fresh,
apt and elegant English made him a model of style. Attention to his tone
of voice also gives a clue to his sense of humour. The Prologue was
composed to be read aloud, and an attempt should be made to read it
aloud in an approximation to the pronunciation, which can be imitated
from one of the several modern recordings that have been made.

PART SIX

CRITICAL HISTORY AND FURTHER READING

HISTORY OF CRITICAL RECEPTION

As Chaucer has been read for six centuries, this is a very brief sketch. In his lifetime he was hailed as *le grand translateur* by Guillaume de Machaut: 'the great translator', that is, of French poems, including *Le Roman de la Rose*.

FIFTEENTH AND SIXTEENTH CENTURY

None of the 400 references to Chaucer in the official records mentions that he was a poet, but on his death he was acknowledged as a master by fifteenth-century poets, notably Hoccleve and Lydgate. The Scots, Henryson, Dunbar and Douglas, regard him as the model of style. *The Canterbury Tales* were printed by William Caxton in 1477 and William Thynne in 1532 and regularly thereafter. Chaucer was always read, but his words became harder to read and his music harder to hear. The first edition to explain how Chaucer's metre worked was Thomas Tyrwhitt's in 1775. At first it was Chaucer's earlier and less realistic work which was admired; he was praised for his wisdom and eloquence. In the sixteenth century Edmund Spenser called Chaucer a 'pure well of English undefyled' and traced English poetic tradition from him. Shakespeare based part of *A Midsummer Night's Dream* on the Knight's Tale.

THE SEVENTEENTH CENTURY

At the end of the seventeenth century *The Canterbury Tales* became more popular than the poet's earlier work. It was praised as giving a representation of the human comedy, not of his day only but of all time. The neo-classical poet and critic John Dryden (1631–1700) wrote: ''Tis sufficient to say according to the proverb, that here is God's plenty. We have our forefathers and great-grand-dames all before us, as they were in Chaucer's days; their general characters are still remaining in mankind, and even in England, though they are called by other names... For mankind is ever the same, and nothing lost out of Nature, though everything is altered.' This seems to fit the General Prologue; Dryden

also wrote a modern version of the Knight's Tale. The first of the
Romantic poets, William Blake (1757–1827), agreed with Dryden's
stress on 'general characters': 'Of Chaucer's characters, as described in
The Canterbury Tales, some of the names or titles are altered by time, but
the characters themselves remain unaltered, and consequently they are
the phisiognomies or lineaments of universal life, beyond which Nature
never steps.'

THE EIGHTEENTH CENTURY
The eighteenth century liked to patronise earlier periods as barbarous and
crude. It admired Chaucer's 'realism' and comedy, and particularly
enjoyed the indecent tales told by the churls in *The Canterbury Tales*. On
Boxing Day, 1801, Dorothy Wordsworth wrote in her journal: 'After tea
we sate by the fire comfortably. I read aloud – The Miller's Tale.' In this
tale, the Miller treats adultery and farting as equally hilarious. The
unmarried Dorothy's choice of text may surprise those who think of the
Wordsworths as solemn and sensitive; the audience were her brother
William and his fiancée. In *The Prelude*, Wordsworth recalls reading the
Reeve's Tale when he was at Cambridge: 'Beside the pleasant Mills of
Trompington / I laughed with Chaucer.'

THE NINETEENTH CENTURY
The Victorians preferred the uplifting, the beautiful, the tragic. Matthew
Arnold judged that Chaucer, though 'free, shrewd, benignant', lacked the
'high seriousness' found in the greatest literature. John Ruskin said that
Chaucer taught the purest theological truth. The Edwardian G.K.
Chesterton, in the last general pre-academic book, *Chaucer* (1932), wrote
well on his Catholicism and his comedy, but turns aside from the cruder
tales which have once more become popular.

MODERN APPROACHES

SCHOLASTICISM
Twentieth-century scholarship was based on Skeat's *Oxford Chaucer*
(1894–7), the first full modern edition; there have been several other
major editions. In the last 100 years the study of Chaucer has continued

in British and American universities, and in the United States has become an academic industry. The approach has been editorial, philological, historical and empirical: the establishment of Chaucer's text, and of the meaning of his words and his references. Chaucer's texts are currently being re-edited electronically from the 80-odd manuscripts of the *Tales*.

The General Prologue was sometimes treated as a source-book for medieval social history. This produced a lot of knowledge, much of it useful. Scholars discovered a hotel-keeper in Southwark in Chaucer's day called Harry Bailly, a Cook called Roger, a ship called the *Maudelayne* in Dartmouth, and an eminent lawyer called Thomas Pynchbec (a possible link with the word *pynch* in the portrait of the Man of Law). This seemed to confirm Chaucer's likeness to the realistic novelists of the nineteenth century and the documentary novelists of the twentieth. In Muriel Bowden's *Commentary* (1957) there is plenty of information about pilgrimages, knights, medieval occupations, the status of a Franklin, the duties of a Manciple or a Summoner, the rules of dress for nuns and guildsmen, an outline of medieval medicine, and how *blankmanger* was made. This information helped with such matters as the sale of pardons, whether nuns were allowed to keep dogs, and the Wife of Bath's habit of wearing coverchiefs on her head on Sundays.

CRITICISM

Criticism until the 1960s was led by historical scholarship and tended to make commonsense assumptions about realism and human continuity, in the tradition of Dryden's 'Here are our fore-fathers...!' In the 1960s, the process of interpreting Chaucerian narrative was influenced by the study of narrative point of view, which had developed in criticism of the novel since the American novelist Henry James. A good example is the work of E.T. Donaldson, who made a still influential distinction between Chaucer the pilgrim and Chaucer the poet (see above, p 57). Chaucer began to be thought of as less of a naïve realist and more of a conscious and rather complicated kind of artist. There was much good criticism of Chaucer in the 1960s and 1970s.

The most notable post-war book on the Prologue is Jill Mann's *Chaucer and Medieval Estates Satire* (1973), which convincingly relates Chaucer's treatment of the pilgrims to the tradition of estates satire. She shows how much he owes to this tradition, but also how he modifies its moralism. She further argues that Chaucer's fascination with and expressed admiration for professional skill and technical expertise, irrespective of the ends to which it is directed, may reflect a moral relativism or indifference. If we think of the Doctor or Lawyer, or the skills with which the Friar and the Pardoner defraud simple lay people, this seems unlikely. But how we read Chaucer's irony is influenced by our presuppositions. One example of misreading is Terry Jones's *Chaucer's Knight*, which saw the portrait of the Knight as wholly ironic, on the grounds that, as he shows, there were no such ideal knights to be found in the 1380s, but only mercenaries. Jones could not take the old ideal seriously and could not believe that Chaucer did. He mistook the tone of the portrait.

LITERARY THEORY

After 1968, literary theory, largely French but imported *via* America, dazzled and dazed the commonsense which underlay British criticism, however intelligent or sophisticated. Believers in structuralism, post-structuralism, deconstruction, new historicism, cultural materialism and of psycho-analytic and feminist approaches challenged the assumptions which had governed interpretation in medieval texts as in others. The competition between these theorised approaches has exposed the pretensions of any idea which claims to control the interpretation of all literary texts. None of these approaches seems to have had much effect on criticism or understanding of the Prologue. An old notion, revived by literary theory, suits Chaucer well: the notion that a text can speak with more than one voice. This approach, associated with the Russian critic Bakhtin, emphasises that some texts are not the product of the author's single voice, and that they are not monologic but **dialogic**, allowing the expression of various points of view.

Interpretation of the Prologue depends very much on whether the focus is on what is conveyed, or on how it is conveyed. In the first case, the content of the portraits will dominate. In the second, the question of Chaucer's irony becomes prominent, and (whether or not we distinguish between the pilgrim and the poet) interpretations will vary. If the operation of irony is admitted, the reader has to interpret, and an historical awareness should come into play. Otherwise the reader's attitude to religion, for example, or to social hierarchy, or to the roles then available to women, may then dominate the views taken of the military, clerical and mercantile portraits, generally or individually. From such a process, Chaucer may emerge as a satirist, a reformer, a more or less humorous comic writer, as a more or less devout Catholic, as a sceptic or a cynic, or as some combination of these. The idea that Chaucer was a cynic seems, to the authors of this Note, untrue to the experience of reading him. On the whole, a focus on content rather than narrative point of view will for most readers be simpler and more enjoyable – as long as it is remembered that Chaucer has a sense of humour.

FURTHER READING

CHAUCER

Piero Boitani and Jill Mann, eds, *The Cambridge Chaucer Companion*, Cambridge University Press, 1986
> Good general introduction by various hands

D.S. Brewer, *Chaucer*, 3rd revised edition, Longman, 1974
> A standard general introduction

John Burrow, ed., *Geoffrey Chaucer: A Critical Anthology*, Penguin, 1969
> An excellent selection of critical comment from early times onwards

– *Essays on Medieval Literature*, Oxford University Press, 1984
> Advanced scholarly criticism

George Kane, *Chaucer*, Oxford University Press, 1984
> A short book by a very experienced scholar

Beryl Rowland, ed., *Companion to Chaucer Studies*, revised edition, Oxford University Press 1979

THE CANTERBURY TALES

Michael Alexander, ed., *The Canterbury Tales: Illustrated Prologue*, Scala Books, 1996
> Text of Prologue with medieval illustrations in colour, including the miniatures of the pilgrims in the Ellesmere manuscript

John J. Anderson, ed., *Chaucer: The Canterbury Tales*, Casebook Series, Macmillan, 1974
>Selected critical articles

Alcuin Blamires, *The Canterbury Tales* (the Critics Debate), London and Atlantic Highlands, NJ, 1987
>A critical selection

Harold Bloom, ed., *The General Prologue to the Canterbury Tales* (Modern Critical Interpretations), Chelsea House, 1991
>Another selection of critical articles

Muriel Bowden, *A Commentary on the General Prologue to the Canterbury Tales*, Macmillan, 1957, 2nd edition 1967
>Full of detailed social history on the pilgrims' professions

Helen Cooper, *The Structure of the Canterbury Tales*, London and Athens, GA, 1983
>Persuasive scholarly criticism

– *The Canterbury Tales* (Oxford Guides to Chaucer), Oxford University Press, 1989
>Comprehensive, up-to-date, well-written and persuasive

Ethelbert Talbot Donaldson, *Speaking of Chaucer*, Athlone Press, 1970
>Elegant and provocative scholarly criticism

Jill Mann, *Chaucer and Medieval Estates Satire*, Cambridge University Press, 1973
>The best recent scholarly book on the tradition inside which Chaucer was writing in the Prologue, and of the ways in which he sophisticated it

Derek Pearsall, *The Canterbury Tales*, Allen and Unwin, 1985
>Useful scholarly commonsense discussions of the whole work

Paul Strohm, *Social Chaucer*, Harvard University Press, 1989
>Well-informed historical scholarship and criticism

RECORDING

The General Prologue, read by Nevill Coghill, Norman Davis, John Burrow, 1982, Argo 1091
>Much the best recording

Events in Europe · Chaucer's life	Literary events
1300 Population of British Isles: *c.*5 million	
1309 Papal See moves to Avignon and comes under French Control	
	1313 Death of Jean de Meun, author of part 2 of *Roman de la Rose*, allegorical poem mocking love, women, the Church and those in authority
	1319 Death of Jean de Joinville, French chronicler
1321 Edward II forced to abdicate, imprisoned and probably murdered; Edward III accedes to throne, with wife Philippa	**1321** Death of Dante Alighieri, author of *Divine Comedy*
	1330 Birth of John Gower, friend of Chaucer and poet
	1331 Birth of William Langland, poet
	1337 Birth of Jean Froissart, who will become Clerk of the Chamber to Queen Philippa, and author of *Chronicles*, a brilliant history of 14th-century western Europe
1338 Beginning of 100 Years War between France and England	
	1341 Petrach crowned as laureate poet at Capitol, Rome
1343-4 Birth of **Geoffrey Chaucer** in London	
1346 French routed at Crécy by Edward III and his son the Black Prince	

Events in Europe	Chaucer's life	Literary events
1349 Black Death reaches England and kills one third of population		
1351 First Statute of Labourers regulates wages in England		
		1353 In Italy, Giovanni Boccaccio finishes his *Decameron*, a collection of 100 tales
1356 English rout French at Poitiers		
	1357 Chaucer in service of Countess of Ulster, wife of Prince Lionel, 3rd son of Edward III	
1359 Edward III makes unsuccessful bid for French throne	**1359** Serves in army in France, under Prince Lionel; taken prisoner	
1360 France cedes a number of territories to England	**1360** Edward III pays ransom of £16 for Chaucer's freedom	
1361 Black Death reappears in England		
1362 English becomes official language in Parliament and Law Courts		
		1363 Birth of Christine de Pisan, French author of *La Cité des Dames*, listing all the heroic acts and virtues of women
	1366 Marries Philippa Pan (or Payne) Roet; in Spain on diplomatic mission	
	1367 Granted life pension for his services to king; birth of his son Thomas; begins travelling abroad on King's business	

Events in Europe	Chaucer's life	Literary events
	1368 On Prince Lionel's death, his services transferred to John of Gaunt, Duke of Lancaster	
	1369 In Picardy with John of Gaunt's expeditionary force; begins *Book of the Duchess* on death of Blanche, John of Gaunt's wife	
	1370-3 Sent on diplomatic missions to Genoa and Florence	**1370 (c)** William Langland's *Piers Plowman* (first version)
	1374 Appointed Controller of the Customs and Subsidy of Wools, Skins and Hides; receives life pension from John of Gaunt	
		1375 (c) *Sir Gawain and the Green Knight* written
	1376 Receives payment for some secret, unspecified service	
1377 Edward III dies and is succeeded by Richard II, son of the Black Prince	**1377** Employed on secret mission to Flanders, and sent to France to negotiate for peace with Charles V	
1378 Beginning of the Great Schism; Urban VI elected Pope in Rome, Clement VII in Avignon	**1378** On diplomatic mission to Lord of Milan	
1380 John Wyclif, who attacked orthodox Church doctrines, condemned as heretic; Wyclif's followers translate Bible into vernacular	**1380** *Parliament of Fowls* written; birth of son Lewis; Cecilia Chaumpayne releases Chaucer from charge of *'de raptu meo'*	**1380s** Religious and 'Mystery' plays popular at this time

Events in Europe	Chaucer's life	Literary events
1381 Peasants' Revolt under Wat Tyler quelled by Richard II		
	1382 Appointed Controller of the Petty Customs	
	1385 Appoints deputy to perform his duties as Controller; writing *Legend of Good Women* and *Troilus and Criseyde*	
	1385-99 Living in Greenwich	
1386 Richard II deprived of power	**1386** Deprived of both official posts; elected Knight of Shire of Kent	
	1387 Wife Philippa dies; begins writing ***The Canterbury Tales***	
	1388 Chaucer sells his pensions to raise money	
1389 Richard II resumes power	**1389** Appointed Clerk of King's Works at Westminster	
		1390 Gower's *Confessio Amantis*
	1391 Writes *Treatise on the Astrolabe* for 'son' Lewis; resigns as Clerk of King's Works and becomes deputy forester of royal forest at North Petherton, Somerset	
1396 John of Gaunt marries his mistress, Katherine (de Roet), Chaucer's sister-in-law		
1399 Richard II forced to abdicate; Henry IV becomes king of England		
1400 Richard II dies in prison; population of British Isles *c*.3.5 million	**1400** Death of Chaucer	**1400 (c)** Arthurian verse romances
		1450 Gutenberg produces first printed book in movable type

allegory saying one thing by means of another (Greek *allos*, other): a way of writing which allows a story to have two different meanings, as in the parables of Jesus in the New Testament; common in spiritual and moral works in the Middle Ages. George Orwell's *Animal Farm* is a modern example

alliteration a sequence of sounds beginning with the same letter (Latin *litera*), usually consonants rather than vowels; common in poetry: 'Around the rugged rocks the ragged rascal ran'

bathos (Greek, sinking) anticlimax, either deliberate or accidental. Chaucer's Merchant was a *worthy man* – but, Chaucer adds, 'to tell the truth I do not know his name'. The Cook is a good cook – but he has an unhealthy ulcer on his leg

chronographia a way of indicating time (Greek *chronos*) in writing (Greek *graph-*), usually by an elaborate circumlocution: 'When Aurora leaves the saffron bed of Tithonus' = at dawn

dialogic a name for a kind of text in which several voices can be heard; the 'dialogue' need not be explicit. (A *monologic* text would express a single viewpoint, the author's.) The word 'dialogic' is taken from the Russian critic, Mikhail Bakhtin

dream-vision a common medieval form in which the author falls asleep and dreams that he sees and describes various personifications and real persons, who talk together and to him. The dreamer seeks to learn from his experiences. Examples are the Old English *Dream of the Rood*, Dante's *Commedia*, Langland's *Piers Plowman* and Chaucer's *Parliament of Fowls*

frame-story outer story containing inset stories, as a picture-frame contains a picture

hyperbole exaggeration, a common figure of speech, as when it is said that the Wife of Bath's head-dress on Sundays weighed ten pounds

image/imagery a verbal representation or picture, either a straightforward description containing a visual element (the Yeoman has *a not heed ... with a broun visage*), or a set of descriptive details making up a more complex image (as in the detailed portrait of the physically violent Miller), or the use of figurative language such as similes and metaphors

irony saying one thing while conveying something else, as when it is said that the Doctor was especially fond of gold because it was an ingredient in medicine

metaphor the description of one thing as another thing. The Miller is described as *a thikke knarre*, or knot of wood. He is not a knot of wood, but has its qualities of impenetrable toughness and awkwardness

metre (Greek *metron*, measure) the simplest quality which distinguishes verse from prose is that it has regular patterns which can be measured or counted. (This does not apply to modern 'free verse'.) 'Metre' can mean verse, or the measure used in a kind of verse. Most English verse has a number of stressed syllables in each line. The metre of Chaucer's Prologue is iambic pentameter rhyming in couplets

parody an imitation of a particular work of literature which makes fun of it by exaggerating or ridiculing its characteristic features

pentameter (Greek, five measures) a line of verse which can be divided into five feet. A foot is a term taken from classical versification (where it means a rhythmical unit with two elements notionally equal in duration) and applied to English verse. But English verse is based not on the length of syllables but on stress, beat or accent; such stresses normally alternate with unstressed syllables. An **iambic pentameter** is a five-beat line beginning with an off-beat

persona fictional personality who speaks in the first person. In some novels, the first-person narrator is clearly not the author. But in Chaucer's poems there is some overlap between the persona and the author, who often writes as if he is reading the poem aloud to his audience

satire the holding up of folly and vice to moral ridicule

simile (Latin *similitudo*, likeness) the likening of one thing to another; comparison using *as* or *like*. Of the Franklin it is said, *Whit was his berd as is the dayeseye*; of the Miller, *His berd as any sowe or fox was reed*

symbol (Greek, putting together) Mark, token, sign

verisimilitude (Latin 'truth-likeness'). The careful imitation of the appearance of reality in a work of fiction; an attribute of literary realism

MARY ALEXANDER has a degree in English from the University of Melbourne and Diplomas in Education from La Trobe University and the Institute of Education, London University. She has taught English in schools in Australia and Britain, and currently teaches A-Level English Literature at St Leonards School in St Andrews, Scotland.

MICHAEL ALEXANDER is Berry Professor of English Literature in the University of St Andrews. He has edited *The Canterbury Tales: The First Fragment* for Penguin, and *The Canterbury Tales: Illustrated Prologue* for Scala Books, and written a York Note on Chaucer's *Knight's Tale*. He has also translated *Beowulf* and other Old English poems into verse for Penguin Classics. He is writing a History of English Literature for Macmillan.